How to Master Life

The Science Behind *The Secret*

Books by Stephen Hawley Martin

Keys to the Kingdom and the Life You Want
(How and why life works
and how it can work for you)

In My Father's House
(A metaphysical thriller in which
the secret of life is revealed)

A Witch in the Family
(What was really behind the Salem witch hunt and the
death of the author's ancestor, Susannah North Martin)

In Tune with the Infinite
(An inspirational masterpiece by Ralph Waldo Trine
with a Foreword by Stephen Hawley Martin)

Death in Advertising
(A whodunit set in an ad agency)

Lean Enterprise Leader
(How to ditch the bureaucracy and create an agile,
lean organization run by empowered teams)

The Color of Demons
(A paranormal thriller written for fun
with his brother David)

For more information, visit www.shmartin.com

How to Master Life

The Science Behind *The Secret*

The Edinburgh Lectures
on Mental Science

by Thomas Troward

and

As a Man Thinketh
by James Allen

Foreword and Afterword
by
Stephen Hawley Martin

THE OAKLEA PRESS

RICHMOND, VIRGINIA

ISBN 13: 978-1-892538-43-7
ISBN 10: 1-892538-43-1

If your bookseller does not have this book in stock,
it can be ordered directly from the publisher.
More information can be found at the
Web site shown below,
or call our toll-free number.

The Oaklea Press
6912-B Three Chopt Road
Richmond, Virginia 23226

Voice: 1-800-295-4066
Email: Info@OakleaPress.com

Web site: http://www.OakleaPress.com

Contents

Foreword

A few individuals down through the ages have known and kept "The Secret" — as it has become known today due to the popular book and movie of that name. A sect of Jews with a bent toward the mystical called the Essenes, who lived in the Middle East from the second century before the current era through the first century, are thought by some scholars to have taught it to Jesus of Nazareth when he was a boy. Though some Christians may not be aware of it, Jesus preached "The Secret" openly — "All things are possible for him who believes" — and he practiced it as expertly as anyone before or since if the miracles recounted in the New Testament are even partially true.

Tradition holds that the Rosicrucian Order passed down "The Secret," also known as the law of attraction, from the time of ancient Egypt to the present day. In the nineteenth and early twentieth centuries, "The Secret" became fairly widely known because of the New Thought Movement that flourished in American and England. The problem for many people, then and now, is internalizing "The Secret" and putting it into practice. They have difficulty believing the law actually works. Doubt, of course, negates the effects of attempts to use the law, and doubters receive what they *believe* they will receive — limited or no results. It seems logical, then, that if how the law works could be explained scientifically — if the mechanics could be determined and revealed — doubts would vanish and results would materialize.

That is the purpose of this book.

To this end, a leader of New Thought named Thomas Troward developed a fascinating and what I believe to be an accurate scientific hypothesis to explain it. Troward presented this at Queens Gate in Edinburgh, Scotland, in 1904, in a series called "The Edinburgh Lectures on Mental Science." Unfortunately, Troward wrote and spoke in the stilted scientific jargon of his day, which made the theory difficult if not impossible for all but the most learned individuals to understand. This has been remedied by the plain English translation of Troward's lectures to be find in this book.

Although Troward's theory is supported by the findings of quantum physics, as will be explained in the Afterword, "The Secret" went underground in the mid to latter part of the twentieth century, largely due I believe to a path of thought taken by the life sciences. This, too, will be discussed.

The wisdom and knowledge of another genius who lived and wrote at the dawn of the twentieth century will be found following Troward's Lectures. It is the magnum opus of Richard Allen, also a leader of the New Thought Movement of a century ago called, *As a Man Thinketh.* This short treatise brings Troward's theory to life by showing how the law manifests in daily life. Each of these two men produced what in my opinion is a *tour de force* of thought and instruction on how we humans can take hold of our lives and steer them where we wish.

Once you have read these masterpieces I believe you will agree it's not too much to say that the knowledge contained in this volume can propel virtually any mentally healthy person, yourself included, to a state not yet achieved by 99.9 percent of the population of this planet. That state is one sought by mental alchemists of every generation and is commonly known as "Mastery of Life."

Troward labeled his field of study "Mental Science," and

he approached it steadfastly from a scientific point of view. No doubt he realized his subject bordered on theology and religion and he took pains not to cross the line. Later generations of scientists have not been so intrepid. After reading Troward's work I think you will agree that modern "Mental Science," the closest thing to which is psychology, does not come close to revealing the secrets Troward lays bear. He set forth fearlessly to answer questions that baffle many scientists today, and he does so quite convincingly.

For example, what is behind the effectiveness of placebos? The placebo effect has been demonstrated time and again in double-blind scientific tests so much so that the phenomenon of patients feeling better after taking inert pills is seen throughout the field of medicine. One report says that after thousands of studies, hundreds of millions of prescriptions and tens of billions of dollars in sales, sugar pills are as effective at treating depression as antidepressants such as Prozac, Paxil and Zoloft.[1] What's more, placebos bring about profound changes in the same areas of the brain these medicines are said to affect — according to this research. For anyone who may have been in doubt or who thought otherwise, this proves that thoughts and beliefs can and do produce physical changes in our bodies.

In addition, the same research reports that placebos often outperform the medicines they're up against. For example, in a trial conducted in April, 2002, comparing the herbal remedy St. John's wort to Zoloft, St. John's wort fully cured 24 percent of the depressed people who received it. Zoloft cured 25 percent. But the placebo fully cured 32 percent.[2]

[1] "Against Depression, a Sugar Pill Is Hard to Beat," by Shankar Vedantam, *The Washington Post,* May 7, 2002.
[2] Ibid.

Taking what one believes to be real medicine sets up the expectation of results, and what a person believes will happen usually does happen. It's been confirmed, for example, that in cultures where belief exists in voodoo or magic, people will actually die after being cursed by a shaman. Such a curse has no power on an outsider who doesn't believe. The expectation causes the result. If you've read my novel, *In My Father's House,* you know I used this phenomenon as a major factor in the plot.

No doubt if Thomas Troward were alive today he'd shrug his shoulders and shake his head, and say something like, "You twenty-first century moderns most surely have lost ground in your knowledge of mental science. The explanation is clear. When thought combined with intention and belief is held in the mind, what else would you expect? Of course placebos work when people think they will. Of course someone who believes he is going to die when cursed will die when cursed."

Read on. After your time with Troward and Allen I'll return to share the findings of a quantum physics experiment that support what they have to say.

Stephen Hawley Martin
March, 2007

The Edinburgh Lectures on Mental Science

by Thomas Troward

(1904)

Edited and language updated for the
twenty-first century reader

by

Stephen Hawley Martin

I. SPIRIT AND MATTER

What is the best way to begin these lectures on Mental Science? The subject can be approached from many sides, each offering some peculiar advantage. After deliberation, it appears to me that the best place to start is with the relationship between Spirit and Matter. The distinction between them — or what we believe to be the distinction — is one we are all familiar with, so I can safely assume everyone will understand. I may, therefore, state this distinction by using the adjectives that we usually apply to distinguish the two — living spirit and dead matter. These terms express what we think is the difference between spirit and matter with sufficient accuracy, and considered only from the point of view of outward appearances this impression is no doubt correct. Mankind is right in trusting the evidence of the senses. Any system that tells us that we are not to do so will never obtain a permanent footing in a sane and healthy community. Nothing is wrong with the evidence conveyed to a healthy mind by the senses of a healthy body. The point where error creeps in is when we come to judge the meaning of this testimony. We are accustomed to judge only by external appearances and by certain limited significances we attach to words. But when we begin to inquire into the real meaning of our words and to analyze the causes that give rise to the appearances, we find our old notions gradually falling away, until at last we realize that we are living in an entirely different world than we formerly recognized. The old limited mode of thought has slipped away, and we discover that we have stepped out into a new order of things where all is liberty and life. This is the work of an enlightened intelligence resulting from persistent determination to discover what truth really is — regardless of preconceived notions. It stems from the determination to think honestly for ourselves rather than let our thinking be done for us. So let us now begin by inquiring what we really mean by "living," which we attribute to spirit, and "dead," which we attribute to matter.

At first we may say that the quality of being alive consists in the power of motion and of being dead in its absence; but a little inquiry into the most recent researches of science will soon show us that this distinction does not go deep enough. It is now a fully established fact of physical science that no atom of what we call "dead matter" is without motion. On the table before me lies a solid lump of steel, but in the light of up-to-date science I know that the atoms of that seemingly inert mass are vibrating with the most intense energy, continually dashing hither and thither, impinging upon and rebounding from one another, or circling round like miniature solar systems, with a ceaseless rapidity whose complex activity is enough to bewilder the imagination. The mass, as a mass, may lie inert upon the table. Nevertheless, it is the location of never-tiring particles in motion with a swiftness to which the speed of an express train is as nothing. It is, therefore, not the mere fact of motion that is at the root of the distinction that we draw instinctively between spirit and matter. We must go deeper. The solution to the problem will never be found by comparing life with what we call dead. The reason for this will become apparent later on. The true key is to be found by comparing one degree of "livingness" with another. There is, of course, one sense in which the quality of livingness cannot be measured in degrees and another sense in which it is entirely a question of degree. We have no doubt that a plant is alive, but we realize that its state of being alive is very different from that of an animal. Again, what average boy would not prefer a fox-terrier to a goldfish for a pet? Or, again, why is it that the boy himself is more advanced than a dog? The plant, the fish, the dog, and the boy are all equally alive. Yet there is a difference in the quality of their livingness about which no one can have any doubt, and no one would hesitate to say that this difference is in the degree of intelligence. In whatever way we turn the subject, we shall always find that what we call the "livingness" of any individual life is ultimately measured by its intelligence. It is the possession of greater intelligence that places the animal higher in the scale of being than the plant, the man higher than the animal, the intellectual man higher than the savage. The increased intelligence calls into activity modes of motion of a higher order. The higher the intelligence, the more completely the mode of motion is under its control; and as we descend in the scale of intelligence, the descent is marked by a corresponding increase in automatic motion not subject to the control of a self-conscious intelligence. This descent is gradual from the expanded self-recognition of the highest human personality to that lowest order of visible forms that we speak of as "things" in which self-recognition is entirely absent.

We see, then, that the livingness of Life consists in intelligence — in other words, in the power of thought. We may therefore say that the distinctive quality of spirit is Thought, and, as the opposite to this, we may say that the distinctive quality of matter is Form. We cannot conceive of matter without form. Some form there must be, even though it may be invisible to the physical eye. For matter to be matter, it must occupy space, and to occupy space necessarily implies a corresponding form. For these reasons we may promulgate a fundamental proposition that the distinctive quality of spirit is Thought and the distinctive quality of matter is Form. This is a radical distinction from which important consequences follow, and should, therefore, be carefully noted.

Form implies the occupation of space and also limitation within certain boundaries. Thought implies neither. When, therefore, we think of Life as existing in any particular form we associate it with the idea of occupying space, so that an elephant may be said to consist of a vastly larger amount of living substance than a mouse. But if we think of Life as the fact of livingness we do not associate it with occupying space, and we at once realize that the mouse is quite as much alive as the elephant, notwithstanding the difference in size. The important point is that if we can conceive of anything as not occupying space, it must be present in its entire totality anywhere and everywhere — that is to say, at every point of space simultaneously.

The scientific definition of time is that it is the period occupied by a body in passing from one given point in space to another, and, therefore, according to this definition, when there is no space there can be no time. Hence the conception of spirit that takes into account that it is devoid of space must also realize that it is devoid of time. We therefore find that the understanding of spirit as pure Thought and not as Form, is the understanding of it as existing independently of time and space. From this it follows that anything that exists on this level must be present in the here and now. In this view, nothing can be remote from us either in time or space: either an idea is entirely dissipated or it exists as a present entity, and not as something that shall be in the future, for where there is no sequence in time there can be no future. Similarly, where no space exists there can be no conception of anything as being at a distance from us. When the elements of time and space are eliminated, all our ideas of things must necessarily be as subsisting in a universal here and an everlasting now. This is, no doubt, a highly abstract conception, but I would ask the student to endeavor to grasp it thoroughly, since it is of vital importance in the practical application of Mental Science, as will appear further on.

The opposite conception is that of things expressing themselves through conditions of time and space, and thus establishing a variety of relations to other things, as of bulk, distance, and direction, or of sequence in time. These two conceptions are respectively the conception of the abstract and the concrete, of the unconditioned and the conditioned, of the absolute and the relative. They are not opposed to each other in the sense of incompatibility, but are each the complement of the other. The only reality is in the combination of the two. The error of the extreme idealist is in trying to realize the absolute without the relative. The error of the extreme materialist is in trying to realize the relative without the absolute. On the one side, the mistake is in trying to realize an inside without an outside, and on the other, in trying to realize an outside without an inside. Both are necessary for anything to exist.

II. THE HIGHER MODE OF INTELLIGENCE CONTROLS THE LOWER

WE have considered the descent from personality, as we know it in ourselves, to matter, as we know it in what we call inanimate forms, and we have seen that this is a gradual descent in the scale of intelligence. This extends from that which is able to realize its own will as tool to make things happen all the way to the form of being that is unable to recognize itself at all. The higher the grade of life, the higher the intelligence. It follows that the supreme principle of Life must also be the ultimate principle of intelligence. This is clearly demonstrated by the grand natural order of the universe. In the light of modern science, the principle of evolution is familiar to us all, and the accurate adjustment existing between all parts of the cosmic scheme is too self-evident to require argument in its favor. Every advance in science consists in discovering new subtleties of connection in this magnificent universal order, which already exists and only needs our recognition to bring it into practical use. If, then, the highest work of the greatest minds consists in nothing else than the recognition of an already existing order, there is no getting away from the conclusion that a paramount intelligence must be inherent in the Life-Principle, which manifests itself as this order. We see, then, that there must be a great cosmic intelligence underlying the totality of things.

The physical history of our planet shows us first an incandescent nebula dispersed over vast infinities of space.

Later this condenses into a central sun surrounded by a family of glowing planets hardly yet consolidated from primordial matter. Untold millenniums of slow geological formation followed. Then, an earth peopled by the lowest forms of life, whether vegetable or animal. From this came the crude beginnings of a majestic, unceasing, unhurried, forward movement that brought things stage by stage to the condition in which we know them now. This steady progression clearly demonstrates the nature of the evolutionary principle. It unerringly provides for the continual advance of the race. But evolution does this by creating such numbers of each kind that, after allowing a wide margin for all possible accidents to individuals, the race shall still continue —

> "So careful of the type it seems
> So careless of the single life."

In short, we may say that the cosmic intelligence works by a Law of Averages that allows a wide margin of accident and failure to the individual.

But the progress towards higher intelligence is always in the direction of narrowing down this margin of accident by taking the individual more and more out of the law of averages, and substituting the law of individual selection. In ordinary scientific language this is the survival of the fittest. The reproduction of fish is on a scale that would choke the sea with them if every individual survived, but the margin of destruction is correspondingly enormous. Thus the law of averages simply keeps up the normal proportion. But at the other end of the scale, reproduction is by no means so enormously in excess of survival. True, accident and disease cut off numbers of human beings before they have gone through the average duration of life, but this is on a very different scale from the premature destruction of hundreds of thousands and the ultimate survival of one. It may, therefore, be taken as an established fact that as intelligence advances the individual ceases to be subject to a mere law of averages and more and more is able to control the likelihood of his own survival.

From this we see that there is a marked distinction between the cosmic intelligence and the individual intelligence. The factor that differentiates the latter from the former is the presence of individual volition. Now the business of Mental Science is to find out the relation of this individual power of volition to the great cosmic law that provides for the maintenance and advancement of the race. The point to be carefully noted is that the power of individual volition is itself the outcome of the cosmic evolutionary principle at the place where it reaches its highest level. The effort of Nature has always been upwards from the time when only the lowest forms of life inhabited the globe, and it has now culminated in the production of a being with a mind capable of abstract reasoning and a brain fitted to be the physical instrument of such a mind. At this stage the all-creating Life-principle reproduces itself in a form capable of recognizing the working of the evolutionary law, and the unity and continuity of purpose running through the whole progression until now indicates that the place of such a being in the universal scheme must be to introduce the operation of that factor which, up to this point, has been conspicuous by its absence — the factor, namely, of intelligent individual volition. The evolution that has brought us up to this standpoint has worked by a cosmic law of averages. It has been a process in which the individual himself has not taken a conscious part.

But because he is what he is and leads the evolutionary procession, if man is to evolve further, it can now only be by his own conscious cooperation with the law that has brought him up to where he is able to realize that such a law exists. His evolution in the future must be by conscious participation in the great work, and this can only be effected by his own individual intelligence and effort. It is a process of intelligent growth. No one else can grow for us: we must each grow for ourselves. This intelligent growth consists in our increasing recognition of the universal law, which has brought us as far as we have yet got, and of our own individual relation to that law, based upon the fact that we ourselves are the most advanced product of it. It is a great maxim that Nature obeys us precisely in proportion as we obey Nature. Let the electrician try to go counter to the principle that electricity must always pass from a higher to a lower potential and he will effect nothing, but let him submit in all things to this one fundamental law, and he can make whatever particular applications of electrical power he will.

These considerations show us that what differentiates the higher from the lower degree of intelligence is the recognition of its own selfhood, and the more intelligent that recognition is, the greater will be the power. The lower degree of self-recognition is that which only realizes itself as an entity separate from all other entities, as the ego distinguished from the non-ego. But the higher degree of self-recognition is that which, realizing its own spiritual nature, sees in all other forms, not so much the non-ego, or that which is not itself, as the alter-ego, or that which is itself in a different mode of expression. Now, it is this higher degree of self-recognition that is the power by which the Mental Scientist produces his results. For this reason it is imperative that he should clearly understand the difference between Form and Being. One is the mode of the relative and the mark of subjection to conditions. The other is the truth of the absolute and is that which controls conditions.

Now this higher recognition of self as an individualization of pure spirit must of necessity control all modes of spirit that have not yet reached the same level of self-recognition. These lower modes of spirit are in bondage to the law of their own being because they do not know the law. Therefore, the individual who has this knowledge can control them through that law. But to understand this we must inquire further into the nature of spirit. I have already shown that the grand scale of adaptation and adjustment of all parts of the cosmic scheme to one another exhibits the presence somewhere of a marvelous intelligence underlying the whole, and the question is, where is this intelligence to be found? Ultimately we can only conceive of it as inherent in some primordial substance that is the root of grosser modes of matter, whether visible, or inferred by science from their effects. It is that power which, in every species and in every individual, becomes that which that species or individual is. Thus we can only conceive of it as a self-forming intelligence inherent in the ultimate substance of which each thing is a particular manifestation. That this primordial substance must be considered as self-forming by an inherent intelligence abiding in itself becomes evident from the fact that intelligence is the essential quality of spirit. If we were to conceive of the primordial substance as something apart from spirit, then we should have to postulate some other power which is neither spirit nor matter, and is the origin of both. This is only putting the idea of a self-evolving power a step further back and asserting the production of a lower grade of undifferentiated spirit by a higher, which is both a purely gratuitous assumption and a contradiction of any idea we can form of undifferentiated spirit at all. However far back, therefore, we may relegate the original starting-point, we cannot avoid the conclusion that, at that point, spirit contains the primary substance in itself. This brings us back to the common statement that it made everything out of nothing. We thus find two factors in the making of all things, Spirit and Nothing. And the addition of Nothing to Spirit leaves only spirit:

$$X + 0 = X.$$

From these considerations we see that the ultimate foundation of every form of matter is spirit, and hence that a universal intelligence exists throughout Nature and is inherent in every one of its manifestations. But this cryptic intelligence does not belong to the particular form. While it may indeed be concentrated into self-recognizing individuality within a physical form, it otherwise lies hidden in that primordial substance of which the visible is an outward manifestation.

This primordial substance is a philosophical necessity. We can picture it as something infinitely finer than the atoms. These themselves are a philosophical inference of physical science. Still, for want of a better word, we may conveniently speak of this primary intelligence inherent in the very substance of things as the atomic intelligence. The term may, perhaps, be open to some objections, but it will serve our present purpose to distinguish this mode of spirit's intelligence from that of the opposite pole, or individual intelligence. This distinction should be carefully noted because it is by the response of the atomic intelligence to the individual intelligence that thought-power is able to produce results on the material plane, as in the cure of disease by mental treatment, and the like. Intelligence manifests itself by responsiveness. The action of the cosmic mind in bringing evolution from its beginning to the present level of human development can be described as a continual intelligent response to the demand each level has made on its environment.

As we have now recognized the presence of a universal intelligence permeating all things, we must also recognize a corresponding responsiveness hidden deep down in the nature of all things that is ready to be called into action when appealed to. All mental treatment depends on this responsiveness of spirit in its lower degrees to the higher degrees of itself. It is here that the difference between the mental scientist and the uninstructed person comes in. The former knows of this responsiveness and makes use of it. The latter cannot use it because he does not know it.

III. THE UNITY OF THE SPIRIT

WE have now paved the way for understanding what is meant by "the unity of the spirit."

The first way we might think about spirit is as the underlying origin of all things. In this we see a universal substance which, at this stage, is not differentiated into any specific forms. Spirit in this instance is not something of the past, not something that existed in a bygone time. Rather, it subsists at every moment of all time in the innermost nature of all being. When we realize this, we see that one form and another that may appear quite different have in common at a deep level an essential unity that acts as the supporter of all the different varieties of forms arising out of it.

As our thought penetrates deeper into the nature of this all-producing spiritual substance we see that it cannot be limited to any one portion of space, but must be limitless as space is, and that the idea of any portion of space where it is not is inconceivable. An intuitive perception the human mind can not get away from is that this primordial, all-generating living spirit must be the size of infinity. We can, therefore, never think of it as anything other than universal or infinite. It is a mathematical truth that the infinite must be a unity. One cannot have two infinities, for then neither would be infinite, each would be limited by the other. Nor can infinity be split into fractions. Mathematically, the infinite is essential unity. This is a point on which too much stress cannot be laid, for important consequences follow from it. As such, unity can be neither multiplied nor divided, for either operation destroys the unity. By multiplying, we produce a plurality of units of the same scale as the original. By dividing, we produce a plurality of units of a smaller scale. A plurality of units is not unity but multiplicity. Therefore, if we would penetrate below the outward nature of the individual to that innermost principle of his being from which his individuality arises, we can do so only by passing beyond individual existence into the unity of universal being. This may appear to be a merely philosophical abstraction, but the student who would produce practical results must realize that these abstract generalizations are the foundation of the practical work he is going to do.

The great fact to be recognized about a unity is that, because it is a single unit, wherever it is located, there too the whole of it must be. The moment we allow our mind to wander off to the idea of extension in space and say that one part of the unit is here and another there, we have descended from the idea of unity into thinking of parts or fractions of a single unit. This is to slip into the idea of a multiplicity of smaller units. In such a case we would be dealing with the relative, or the relation existing between two or more entities, and so have passed out of the region of simple unity or absolute. It is, therefore, a mathematical necessity that, because the originating Life-principle is infinite, it is a single unit, and consequently, wherever it is at all, the whole of it must be present. But because it is infinite, or limitless, it is everywhere, and therefore it follows that the whole of spirit must be present at every point in space at the same moment. Spirit is thus omnipresent in its entirety, and it is accordingly correct, logically, that at every moment of time all spirit is concentrated at any point in space that we may choose to fix our thought upon. This is the fundamental fact of all being, and it is for this reason that I have prepared the way for it by laying down the relation between spirit and matter as that between idea and form, on the one hand the absolute from which the elements of time and space are entirely absent, and on the other the relative that is entirely dependent on those elements. This great fact is that pure spirit continually subsists in the absolute, whether in a corporeal body or not in a corporeal body, and from it flows the phenomena of being, whether on the mental plane or on the physical. The knowledge of this fact regarding spirit is the basis of all conscious spiritual operation. Therefore, as our recognition of it grows, so in proportion will grow our power of producing outward visible results by the action of our thoughts. The whole is greater than its part, and therefore, if, by our recognition of this unity we can concentrate all spirit into any given point at any moment, we thereby include any individualization of it that we may wish to deal with. The practical importance of this conclusion is too obvious to need enlarging upon.

Pure spirit is Life viewed separately from the matrix that embodies it in a particular form in time and space. In this aspect it is pure intelligence undifferentiated into individuality. As pure intelligence it is in infinite responsiveness and susceptibility. Devoid of any relation to time and space, it is also devoid of individual personality. It is, therefore, in this aspect a purely impersonal element upon which, by reason of its inherent intelligence and susceptibility, we can impress any recognition of personality that we will.

These are the great facts that the mental scientist works with, and the student will do well to ponder deeply on their significance and on the responsibilities which their realization must necessarily carry with it.

IV. SUBJECTIVE AND OBJECTIVE MIND

UP TO THIS point it has been necessary to lay the foundations of the science by the statement of highly abstract general principles that we have reached by purely metaphysical reasoning. We now pass on to the consideration of certain natural laws which have been established by a long series of experiments and observations, the full meaning and importance of which will become clear when we see their application to the general principles that have been discussed up until now. The phenomena of hypnosis are now so fully recognized as established scientific facts that it is quite superfluous to discuss the question of their credibility. Two great medical schools have been founded upon them, and in some countries they have become the subject of special legislation. The question before us at the present day is, not as to the credibility of the facts, but as to the proper inferences to be drawn from them. A correct understanding of these inferences is one of the most valuable aids to the mental scientist, for it confirms the conclusions of purely a priori reasoning. It does so by an array of experiments that places the correctness of those conclusions beyond doubt.

The great truth which the science of hypnotism has brought to light is the dual nature of the human mind. Much conflict exists between different writers as to whether this duality results from the presence of two actually separate minds in the one man, or in the action of the same mind in the employment of different functions. This is one of those distinctions without a difference that are so often an obstacle to seeing the truth. A man must be a single individuality to be a man at all, and, so, the net result is the same whether we conceive of his varied modes of mental action as proceeding from a set of separate minds strung, so to speak, on the thread of his one individuality and each adapted to a particular use, or as varied functions of a single mind. In either case we are dealing with a single individuality. How we may picture the inner workings of the mental mechanism is merely a question of what picture will bring into focus the nature of its action most clearly. Therefore, as a matter of convenience, I shall in these lectures speak of this dual action as though it proceeded from two minds, an outer and an inner. The inner mind we will call the subjective mind and the outer the objective, by which names the distinction is most frequently indicated in literature on the subject.

A long series of careful experiments by highly-trained observers, some of them men of worldwide reputation, has fully established certain remarkable differences between the action of the subjective and that of the objective mind. These may be briefly stated as follows. The subjective mind is only able to reason deductively. It cannot reason not inductively. On the other hand, the objective mind can do both.

Inductive reasoning is to progress from result to cause, step by step, logically. For example, a detective called in to fathom the mystery of a crime would look upon the result, the finished deed, and by reasoning backward endeavor to tell just how the crime was committed as well as when it was committed and by whom. This is inductive reasoning.

Deductive reasoning, on the other hand, is done from the cause forward to its ultimate end instead of backward to the cause. Deductive reasoning embraces no question, no analysis, no examination, but is a mere chain of subsequent actions, each a logical result of the former. It is the kind reasoning that a criminal may use in committing a crime. The criminal may walk into a room, for example, and see a man counting his money. He might reason somewhat as follows: "I need money. There is plenty of it. I need some or all of that, so I will take it. The man counting it is protecting the money. Therefore, I will get rid of the man and then take the money. To get rid of the man I will kill him. To kill him I will shoot him. I will use my revolver. I will use my revolver to shoot him in the back. He will drop to the floor. He will be unconscious, He will die. I will take the money and run. I will get out of the window through which I came."

This is to reason deductively.

The relation of the two modes of reasoning is that, first by observing a sufficient number of instances, we inductively reach the conclusion that a certain principle is generally true, and then we enter upon the deductive process by assuming the truth of this principle and determining what result must follow in a particular case on the hypothesis of its truth. Thus deductive reasoning proceeds on the assumption of the correctness of certain hypotheses or suppositions that it starts out with. It is not concerned with the truth or falsity or morality of those suppositions, but only with the question as to what results must necessarily follow based on the supposition they are true.

Inductive reasoning, on the other hand, is the process by which we compare a number of separate instances with one another until we see the common factor that gives rise to them all. Induction proceeds by the comparison of facts, and deduction by the application of universal principles.

Only the deductive method is employed by the subjective mind. Countless experiments on persons in the hypnotic state have shown that the subjective mind is utterly incapable of making the selection and comparison necessary to the inductive process. It will accept any suggestion, however false. Having once accepted a suggestion, it is strictly logical in deducing the proper conclusions from it, working out every suggestion to the smallest fraction of the results which flow from it.

As a consequence of this it follows that the subjective mind is entirely under the control of the objective mind. With the utmost fidelity it reproduces and works out to its final consequences whatever the objective mind impresses upon it. The facts of hypnotism show that ideas can be impressed on the subjective mind by the objective mind of another as well as by that of its own. This is a most important point, for it is on this amenability to suggestion by the thought of another that all the phenomena of healing, whether present or absent, of telepathy and the like, depend. Under the control of the practiced hypnotist the very personality of the subject becomes changed for the time being. He believes himself to be whatever the operator tells him he is — he is a swimmer breasting the waves, a bird flying in the air, a soldier in the tumult of battle, an Indian stealthily tracking his victim. In short, for the time being, he identifies himself with any personality that is impressed upon him by the will of the operator, and he acts the part with inimitable accuracy.

The experiments of hypnotism go further and show the existence in the subjective mind of powers far transcending any exercised by the objective mind through the medium of the physical senses. These include thought-reading, thought-transference, clairvoyance, and the like, all of which are frequently manifested when the patient is brought into the higher mesmeric state. This is experimental proof of the existence in ourselves of transcendental faculties, the full development and conscious control of which would place us in a perfectly new sphere of life.

But it should be noted that the control must be our own and not that of any external intelligence, whether in the flesh or out of it. But perhaps the most important fact which hypnotic experiments have demonstrated is that the subjective mind is the builder of the body. The subjective entity in the patient is able to diagnose the character of the disease from which he is suffering and to point out suitable remedies, indicating a physiological knowledge exceeding that of the most highly trained physicians, and also a knowledge of the correspondences between diseased conditions of the bodily organs and the material remedies which can give relief. From this it is only a step further to those many instances in which it entirely dispenses with the use of material remedies and works itself directly on the organism, so that complete restoration to health follows as the result of the suggestions of perfect soundness made by the operator to the patient while in the hypnotic state.

Now these are facts fully established by hundreds of experiments conducted by a variety of investigators in different parts of the world, and from them we may draw two inferences of the highest importance: 1.) that the subjective mind is in itself absolutely impersonal, and 2.) that it is the builder of the body, or in other words it is the creative power in the individual.

That it is impersonal in itself is shown by its readiness to assume any personality the hypnotist chooses to impress upon it; and the unavoidable inference is that its realization of personality proceeds from its association with the particular objective mind of its own individuality. Whatever personality the objective mind impresses upon it, that personality it assumes and acts up to. Since it is the builder of the body, it will build up a body in correspondence with the personality thus impressed upon it.

These two laws of the subjective mind form the foundation of the axiom that our body represents the aggregate of our beliefs. If our fixed belief is that the body is subject to all sorts of influences beyond our control, and that this, that, or the other symptom shows that such and such an uncontrollable influence is at work on us, then this belief is impressed upon the subjective mind, and the subjective mind by the law of its nature accepts it without question and proceeds to fashion bodily conditions in accordance with the belief. Again, if our fixed belief is that certain material remedies are the only means of cure, then we find in this belief the foundation of all medicine. There is nothing unsound in the theory of medicine. It is the strictly logical correspondence with the measure of knowledge that those who rely on it are as yet able to assimilate, and it acts accurately in accordance with their belief that in a large number of cases medicine will do good, but also in many instances it fails. Therefore, for those who have not yet reached a more nonphysical perception of the law of nature, the healing agency of medicine is a most valuable aid to the alleviation of physical maladies. The erroneous thinking to be fought against is not the belief that, in its own way, medicine is capable of doing good, but the belief that there is no higher or better way.

Then, on the same principle, if we realize that the subjective mind is the builder of the body, and that the body is subject to no other influences besides those that reach it through the subjective mind, then what we have to do is impress this upon the subjective mind and habitually think of it as a fountain of perpetual Life. It should be regarded as a spring or source that is continually renovating the body by building strong, healthy material. We need to use our objective mind to impress upon our subjective mind that it does all this independently of any influences of any sort, except those of our own desire.

Once we fully grasp this realization, we shall see that it is just as easy to externalize healthy conditions of body as it is the contrary. In a practical sense, the process amounts to a belief in our own power of life, and since this belief, if thoroughly held by us, must produce a correspondingly healthy body, we should spare no pains to convince ourselves that there are sound and reasonable grounds for holding it. To make a solid case for this conviction is one purpose of Mental Science.

V. FURTHER CONSIDERATIONS REGARDING SUBJECTIVE AND OBJECTIVE MIND

CONSIDERATION of the phenomena of hypnotism will show that what we call the hypnotic state is the normal state of the subjective mind. The subjective mind always conceives of itself in accordance with a suggestion conveyed to it, either consciously or unconsciously in concert with the manner of objective mind that governs it. Accordingly, the subjective mind gives rise to corresponding external results. Abnormal conditions can be induced by hypnotism because of the removal of the usual control held by an individual's own objective mind over his subjective mind. In this case, another control is substituted.

Thus we may say that the normal characteristic of the subjective mind is its perpetual action in accordance with some sort of suggestion. It becomes therefore a question of the highest importance to determine in every case what the nature of the suggestion shall be and from what source it shall proceed. Before considering the sources of suggestion, however, we must understand more fully the place occupied by subjective mind in the order of Nature.

If the student has followed what has been said regarding the presence of intelligent spirit pervading all space and permeating all matter, he will now have little difficulty recognizing this all-pervading spirit as universal subjective mind. That it cannot as universal mind have the qualities of objective mind is obvious. The universal mind is the creative power throughout Nature. As the originating power, it must first give rise to the various forms in which objective mind recognizes its own individuality. Only then can these individual minds react upon it. Hence, as pure spirit or first cause, it cannot possibly be anything else than subjective mind. The fact has been abundantly proved by experiment that the subjective mind is the builder of the body. This demonstrates that the power of creating by growth from within is the essential characteristic of the subjective mind. Hence, both from experiment and from a priori reasoning, we may say that wherever we find creative power at work, there we are in the presence of subjective mind — whether it is working on the grand scale of the cosmos, or on the miniature scale of the individual. We may therefore lay it down as a principle that the universal all-permeating intelligence, which has been considered in the second and third sections, is purely subjective mind, and therefore follows the law of subjective mind — namely that it is amenable to any suggestion and will carry out any suggestion that is impressed upon it to its most rigorously logical consequences.

The incalculable importance of this truth may not perhaps strike the student at first, but a little consideration will show him the enormous possibilities that are stored in it. In the concluding section I shall touch briefly upon the very serious conclusions resulting from it. For the present it will be sufficient to realize that the subjective mind in ourselves is the same subjective mind that is at work throughout the universe giving rise to the infinite number of natural forms that surrounded us. In like manner it gives rise to each of us.

It may be called the supporter of our individuality. We may loosely speak of our individual subjective mind as our personal share in the universal mind. This, of course, does not imply the splitting up of the universal mind into fractions. It is to avoid this error that I have discussed the essential unity of spirit in the third section. Nevertheless, in order to avoid highly abstract concepts in the present stage of the student's progress, as a matter of convenience let us employ the idea of a personal share in the universal subjective mind.

To understand our individual subjective mind in this manner will help us overcome the great metaphysical difficulty that meets us in our efforts to make conscious use of first cause — in other words, to create external results by the power of our own thought. Ultimately there can be only one first cause, the universal mind, but because it is universal it cannot, as universal, act on the plane of the individual and particular. For it to do so would be for it to cease to be universal and therefore cease to be the creative power that we wish to employ. On the other hand, the fact that we are working for a specific definite objective implies our intention to use this universal power for a particular purpose. Thus we find ourselves involved in the paradox of seeking to make the universal act on the plane of the particular. We want to effect a junction between the two extremes of Nature, the innermost creative spirit and a particular external form. Between these two is a great gulf, and the question is how it can be bridged.

That our individual subjective mind is our personal share in the universal subjective mind affords the means of overcoming this difficulty. On the one hand, it is in immediate connection with the universal mind. On the other, it is in immediate connection with the individual objective, or intellectual mind. This in turn is in immediate connection with the external world, which is conditioned in time and space.

Thus the relationship between the subjective and objective minds in an individual person forms the bridge that is needed to connect the two extremities.

The individual subjective mind may therefore be regarded as the organ of the Absolute in precisely the same way that the objective mind is the organ of the Relative. In order to regulate our use of these two organs it is necessary to understand what the terms "absolute" and "relative" actually mean. The absolute is that which contemplates itself as existing in itself and not in relation to something else. It is all-encompassing. The relative is that which contemplates itself as related to other things, that is to say as surrounded by a certain environment. The absolute is the region of causes. The relative is the region of conditions. Hence, if we wish to control conditions, we can do so by our thought-power operating on the plane of the absolute, and this it can do only through the medium of the subjective mind.

Conscious use of the creative power of thought can be achieved by Thinking in the Absolute. This can only be attained by a clear conception of the interaction between our different mental functions. For this purpose the student cannot too strongly impress upon himself that subjective mind, on whatever scale, is intensely sensitive to suggestion. As a creative power the subjective mind works to externalize accurately that suggestion that is most deeply impressed upon it. We can take any idea out of the realm of the relative, where it is limited and restricted by conditions imposed upon it through surrounding circumstances, and transfer it to the realm of the absolute where it is not thus limited. By a clearly defined method, the correct recognition of our mental makeup will enable us to do this.

We first think of what we want in a way that relates to existing circumstances. These circumstances may, or may not, appear favorable in this regard. We want to eliminate chance and attain something certain. For this to happen, we must work on the plane of the absolute. To do so we must endeavor to impress upon our subjective mind the idea or concept of our desire quite apart from any conditions. This separation from conditions implies the elimination of the idea of time, and consequently *we must think of the thing as already in actual existence.* Unless we do this we are not operating upon the plane of the absolute, and therefore are not employing the creative power of our thought.

The simplest practical method of gaining the habit of thinking in this manner is to conceive the existence in the spiritual world of a spiritual prototype of every existing thing, which becomes the root of the corresponding external existence. If we habitually look on the spiritual prototype as the essential being of the thing, and the material form as the growth of this prototype into outward expression, then we shall see that the initial step in producing any external fact must be the creation of its spiritual prototype. This prototype, being purely spiritual, can be formed only by thought.

In order to have substance on the spiritual plane, whatever we wish to create must be thought of as actually existing there. This idea was elaborated on by Plato in his doctrine of archetypical ideas, and by Swedenborg in his doctrine of correspondences. A still greater teacher said, "All things whatsoever ye pray and ask for, believe that ye have received them, and ye shall receive them." (Mark XI. 24, R.V.)

The difference of the tenses in this passage is remarkable. The speaker bids us first to believe that our desire has already been fulfilled, that it is a thing already accomplished, then that its accomplishment will follow as a thing in the future. This is nothing less than an explicit direction for making use of the creative power of thought by impressing upon the universal subjective mind the particular thing that we desire as an already existing fact. In following this direction we are thinking on the plane of the absolute and in so doing we eliminate from our minds all consideration of conditions, which imply limitation and the possibility of adverse contingencies. We are thus planting a seed that, if left undisturbed, will infallibly germinate into external fruition.

By thus making intelligent use of our subjective mind, we create a nucleus, so to speak. This nucleus is no sooner created than it begins to exercise an attractive force, drawing to itself material of a like character to its own. If this process is allowed to continue undisturbed, it will persist until an external form that corresponds to the nature of the nucleus comes into being on the objective plane. This is in fact the universal method of Nature on every plane.

Some of the most advanced thinkers in modern physical science, in the endeavor to probe the great mystery of the first origin of the world, have postulated the formation of what they call "vortex rings" formed from an infinitely fine primordial substance. They tell us that if such a ring is formed on the smallest scale and then set to rotating, it would be moving in pure ether and subject to no friction. Therefore it must, according to all known laws of physics, be indestructible and its motion perpetual. Let two such rings approach each other, and by the law of attraction, they would coalesce into a whole, and so on until manifested matter as we apprehend it with our external senses, is formed at last. Of course no one has ever seen these rings with the physical eye. They are one of those abstractions that result if we follow out the observed laws of physics and the unavoidable sequences of mathematics to their necessary consequences. We cannot account for the things that we can see unless we assume the existence of other things that we cannot see. The "vortex theory" is one of these assumptions. This theory has not been put forward by mental scientists but by purely physical scientists. The conclusion they reached is that all the innumerable forms of Nature have their origin in the infinitely minute nucleus of the vortex ring. This occurred by whatever means the vortex ring may have received its initial impulse, a question with which physical science, as such, is not concerned.

As the vortex theory accounts for the formation of the inorganic world, so does biology account for the formation of the living organism. That also has its origin in a primary nucleus which, as soon as it is established, operates as a center of attraction for the formation of all those physical organs of which the perfect individual is composed. The science of embryology shows that this rule holds good without exception throughout the whole range of the animal world, including man. Botany shows the same principle at work throughout the vegetable world. All branches of physical science demonstrate the fact that every completed manifestation, of whatever kind and on whatever scale, began with the establishment of a nucleus, infinitely small but endowed with an unquenchable energy of attraction that caused it to steadily increase in power and sureness of purpose, until the process of growth is completed and the matured form is an accomplished fact.

If this is the universal method of Nature, nothing is unnatural in supposing that it must begin its operation at a stage further back than the formation of the nucleus in material form. As soon as the nucleus is called into being it begins to operate by the law of attraction on the material plane. The question is, what is the force that originates the material nucleus?

A recent work in physical science provides the answer: "In its ultimate essence, energy may be incomprehensible by us except as an exhibition of the direct operation of that which we call Mind or Will."

The quotation is from a course of lectures on "Waves in Water, Air and Ether," delivered in 1902, at the Royal Institution, by J. A. Fleming.

Here, then, is the testimony of physical science that the originating energy is Mind or Will. We are, therefore, not only making a logical deduction from unavoidable intuitions of the human mind, we are also following along the lines of the most advanced physical science when we say that the action of Mind plants that nucleus which, if allowed to grow undisturbed, will eventually attract to itself all that is necessary for its manifestation in outward visible form.

Now, the only action of Mind is Thought. It is for this reason that our thoughts create corresponding external conditions. Our thoughts create the nucleus that attracts to itself its own correspondences in due order until the finished work is manifested on the external plane. This is according to the strictly scientific conception of the universal law of growth.

We may therefore briefly sum up the argument made in this section by saying that our thought of anything forms a spiritual prototype of it. This prototype in effect is a nucleus

41

or center of attraction for the conditions necessary for whatever we have so constructed on the spiritual plane to eventually manifest on the material plane. This happens in accordance with a law of growth that is inherent in the prototype itself.

VI. THE LAW OF GROWTH

A CORRECT understanding of the law of growth is of the highest importance to the student of Mental Science. The great fact to be realized regarding Nature is that it is natural. We may pervert the order of Nature, but it will prevail in the long run, returning, as Horace says, by the back door even though we drive it out with a pitchfork. The beginning, middle and end of the law of Nature is the principle of growth from a vitality that exists in the entity itself. If we understand this thoroughly we shall not undo our own work by trying to force things to become that which, by their own nature, they are not. When the Bible says that "he who believeth shall not make haste," it is enunciating a great natural principle that success depends on our using, and not opposing, the universal law of growth.

No doubt the greater the vitality we put into the germ, which we have agreed to call the spiritual prototype, the quicker it will germinate. This is simply because by creating a more fully developed mental concept we put more growing power into the seed than we do by a feebler conception. Our mistakes always eventually resolve themselves into distrusting the law of growth. We may think we can hasten growth by some exertion of our own from without, and are thus led into hurry and anxiety, not to say sometimes into the employment of grievously wrong methods. Or we may give up all hope and so deny the germinating power of the seed we have planted. The result in either case is the same, for in either case we are in effect forming a fresh spiritual prototype of an opposite character to our desire, which therefore neutralizes the one first formed. The new disintegrates the original and usurps its place. The law is always the same, that our Thought forms a spiritual prototype which, if left undisturbed, will reproduce itself in external circumstances; the only difference is in the sort of prototype we form, and thus evil is brought to us by precisely the same law as good.

These considerations will greatly simplify our idea of life. We have no longer to consider two forces. Only one is the cause of all things. The difference between good and evil has to do simply with the direction this force is made to flow. It is a universal law that if we reverse the action of a cause, we at the same time reverse the effect. We can apply motion to an apparatus to generate electricity, or use electricity and the same apparatus to generate motion. Or, to use an example from arithmetic, if 10 divided by 2 equals 5, then 10 divided by 5 equals 2. Therefore, once we recognize the power of thought to produce any results at all, we should see that the law by which negative thought produces negative results is the same law by which positive thought produces positive results.

All our distrust of the law of growth, whether shown in the anxious endeavor to bring pressure to bear from without, or in allowing despair to take the place of cheerful expectation, is reversing the action of the original cause and consequently reversing the nature of the results. It is for this reason that the Bible, which is the most deeply occult of all books, continually lays so much stress upon the efficacy of faith and the destructive influence of unbelief. In like manner, all books on every branch of spiritual science emphatically warn us against the admission of doubt or fear. They are the inversion of the principle that builds up, and are therefore the principle that pulls down. The Law itself never changes, and it is on the unchangeableness of the law that all Mental Science is founded.

We are accustomed to accept as fact the unchangeable nature of natural law in our every day life. It should therefore not be difficult to realize that the same unchangeable nature of law that we accept on the visible side of nature is just as unchangeable on the invisible side. The variable factor is not the law but our own will. By combining the variable factor of our will with the invariable factor of natural law, we can produce whatever results we desire.

Since the principle of growth is that of inherent vitality in the seed itself, the operations of the gardener have their exact parallel in Mental Science. Perhaps we do not put the self-expansive vitality into the seed. Nevertheless, we must sow it, and we may also water it, so to speak, by quiet concentrated contemplation of our desire as an actually accomplished fact. In so doing we must carefully remove any idea of a strenuous effort on our part to make the seed grow. Our contemplation's effectiveness is in helping to keep out those negative thoughts of doubt, which would plant tares among our wheat, and therefore, instead of anything of effort, such contemplation should be accompanied by a feeling of pleasure and restfulness in foreseeing the certain accomplishment of our desires. This is analogous to making our requests known to God with thanksgiving, as recommended by St. Paul. It has its reason in that perfect wholeness of the Law of Being which only needs our recognition of it to be used by us to any extent we wish.

Some people possess the power of visualization, or making

mental pictures of things, to a greater degree than others. This faculty may be employed advantageously to facilitate the working of the Law. But those who do not possess this faculty in any marked degree, need not be discouraged by their lack of it. Visualization is not the only way to put the law to work on the invisible plane. Those whose mental bias is towards physical science should realize this Law of Growth as the creative force throughout all nature. Those who have a mathematical turn of mind may reflect that all solids are generated from the movement of a point, which, as our old friend Euclid tells us, is that which has no parts nor magnitude, and is therefore as complete an abstraction as any spiritual nucleus could be.

To use the apostolic words, we are dealing with the substance of things not seen, and we have to attain that habit of mind by which we shall see its reality and feel that we are mentally manipulating the only substance there ultimately is. All visible things are simply different manifestations of this substance. We must therefore regard our mental creations as spiritual realities and then implicitly trust the Laws of Growth to do the rest.

VII. RECEPTIVITY

IN order to lay the foundations for practical work, the student must do his best to get a clear conception of what is meant by the intelligence of undifferentiated spirit. To do so, we need to grasp the idea of intelligence apart from anything that may give it individuality. The ability to do so is rather apt to elude us until we grow accustomed to the idea of an intelligence that is unattached to any particular entity or thing. The failure to realize this quality of spirit has given rise to all the theological errors that have brought bitterness into the world. This failure has also been prominent among the causes that have retarded the real and true development of mankind.

To accurately convey this conception in words is perhaps impossible, and to attempt to place a definition on it is to introduce that very idea of limitation that we are trying to avoid. It is a matter of feeling rather than of definition. Yet some endeavor must be made to indicate the direction in which we must feel for this great truth if we are to find it.

The idea is that of realizing personality without the selfhood that differentiates one person from another. "I am not that other because I am myself," is the definition of individual selfhood. This necessarily imparts the idea of limitation. The recognition of any other individual at once affirms a point at which our own individuality ceases to exist and the other begins. This manner of recognition cannot be attributed to the Universal Mind. For it to recognize a point where itself ceased and something else began would be to recognize itself as not universal.

The very meaning of universality is the inclusion of all things. Therefore, for this intelligence to recognize anything as being outside itself would be a denial of its own being. We may therefore say without hesitation that, whatever may be the nature of its intelligence, it must be entirely devoid of the element of self-recognition as an individual personality on any scale whatsoever. Seen in this light, it is at once clear that the originating all-pervading Spirit is the grand impersonal principle of Life, which gives rise to all the particular manifestations of Nature. Its absolutely impersonal character, in the sense of the entire absence of any consciousness of individual selfhood, is a point on which it is impossible to insist too strongly.

The attributing of an impossible individuality to the Universal Mind is one of the two grand errors that we find in all ages sapping the foundations of religion and philosophy. The other consists in rushing to the opposite extreme and denying the quality of personal intelligence to the Universal Mind.

The answer to this error remains, as of old, in the simple question, "He that made the eye shall He not see? He that planted the ear shall He not hear?" Or, to use a popular proverb, "You cannot get out of a bag more than there is in it."

Consequently, the fact that we ourselves are centers of personal intelligence is proof that the infinite, from which these centers are concentrated, must be infinite intelligence. Thus we cannot avoid attributing to the infinite the two factors that constitute personality, namely, intelligence and will. We are therefore brought to the conclusion that this universally diffused essence, that we may think of as spiritual protoplasm, must possess all the qualities of personality without that conscious recognition of self that constitutes separate individuality.

Since the word "personality" has became so associated in our ordinary talk with the idea of "individuality," it will perhaps be better to coin a new word. In doing so, we might speak of the "personal-ness" of the Universal Mind as indicating its personal quality, apart from individuality. We must realize that this universal spirit permeates all space and all manifested substance, just as physical scientists tell us that the ether does, and that wherever it is, there it must carry with it all that it is in its own being. We shall see then that we are in the middle of an ocean of undifferentiated yet intelligent Life. This Life is above, below, and all around. It permeates ourselves both mentally and corporeally, and it permeates all other beings as well.

Gradually, as we come to realize the truth of this statement, our eyes will begin to open to the immense significance associated with it, i.e. all Nature is pervaded by an interior personal-ness, infinite in its potentialities of intelligence, responsiveness, and power of expression. It is only waiting to be called into activity by our recognition of it.

By the terms of its nature this infinitely potent personal-ness can respond to us only as we recognize it. If we are at that intellectual level where we can see nothing but chance governing the world, then this underlying universal mind will present to us nothing but a fortuitous confluence of forces without any intelligible order. On the other hand, if we are sufficiently advanced to see that such a confluence could only produce a chaos, and not a cosmos, then our conceptions expand to the idea of universal Law, and we find this to be the nature of the all-underlying principle. We will have made an immense advance from the realm of mere accident into a new world where definite principles exist that we can count on with absolute certainty. But here is the crucial point. The laws of the universe are there, but if we are ignorant of them they can do us no good.

Only through experience gained by repeated failure can we get any insight into the laws with which we have to deal. How painful each step and how slow the progress! Eons upon eons would not suffice to grasp all the laws of the universe in their totality, not in the visible world only, but also in the world of the unseen. Each failure to know the true law implies suffering arising from our ignorant breaking of it. And since Nature is infinite, we are met by the paradox that we must in some way try to encompass the knowledge of the infinite with our individual intelligence. We must perform a pilgrimage along an unceasing Via Dolorosa beneath the lash of the inexorable Law until we find the solution to the problem.

It will be asked, "May we not go on until at last we attain the possession of all knowledge?" People do not realize what is meant by "the infinite," or they would not ask such questions. The infinite is that which is limitless and exhaustless. Imagine the vastest capacity you will, and having filled it with the infinite, what remains of the infinite is just as infinite as before. To the mathematician this may be put very clearly. Raise X to any power you will, and however vast may be the disparity between it and the lower powers of X, both are equally incommensurate with it. The universal reign of Law is a magnificent truth. It is one of the two great pillars of the universe symbolized by the two pillars that stood at the entrance to Solomon's temple: it is Jachin, but Jachin must be brought into balance by Boaz.

It is an enduring truth, which can never be altered, that every infraction of the Law of Nature must carry consequences with it. We can never get beyond the range of cause and effect. There is no escaping from the law of punishment, except by knowledge. If we know a law of Nature and work with it, we shall find it our unfailing friend, ever ready to serve us, and never rebuking us for past failures. But if we ignorantly or willfully transgress it, it is our implacable enemy, until we again become obedient to it. Therefore, the only redemption from perpetual pain and servitude is through self growth to the point at which we can grasp infinitude itself.

How is this to be accomplished? It is to be done by our progress to that kind and degree of intelligence by which we realize the inherent personal-ness of the divine all-pervading Life, which is at once the Law and the Substance of all that is. The Jewish rabbis of old said, "The Law is a Person." When we realize that universal Life and universal Law are one with universal Personal-ness, then we will have established the pillar Boaz as the needed complement to Jachin. When we find the common point in which these two unite, we have raised the Royal Arch through which we may triumphantly enter the Temple. We must dissociate the Universal Personal-ness from every conception of individuality. The universal can never be the individual — that would be a contradiction in terms. But because the universal personal-ness is the root of all individual personalities, it finds its highest expression in response to those who realize its personal nature. And it is this recognition that solves the seemingly insoluble paradox. The only way to attain knowledge of the Infinite Law that can change the Via Dolorosa into the Path of Joy is to embody in ourselves a principle of knowledge proportional to the infinite that is to be known. This is accomplished by realizing that we are points of conscious awareness floating in a living, limitless ocean of universal Intelligence. This Intelligence is without individual personality, but in producing us it concentrates itself into the individual personalities that we are.

What should be the relation of such an intelligence towards us? Not one of favoritism. The Law cannot respect one person above another. It itself is the root and support for each one of us alike. Not one of refusal to our advances. Without individuality it can have no personal objective of its own to conflict with ours. In addition, since it is itself the origin of all individual intelligence, it cannot be shut off by inability to understand. By the very terms of its being, therefore, this infinite, underlying, all-producing Mind must be ready in an instant to respond to all who realize their true relation to it.

As the very principle of Life itself it must be infinitely susceptible to feeling, and consequently it will reproduce with absolute accuracy whatever conception of itself we impress upon it. Hence, if we realize the human mind as being that stage in the evolution of the cosmic order at which an individuality has arisen capable of expressing, not merely the livingness, but also the personal-ness of the universal underlying spirit, then we see that its most perfect manner of self-expression must be by identifying itself with these individual personalities.

The identification is, of course, limited by the quality and quantity of the individual intelligence of the personality. By this is meant not merely the intellectual perception of the sequence of cause and effect, but also that indescribable reciprocity of feeling by which we instinctively recognize something in another that makes that person akin to ourselves. When we realize that the innermost principle of being — this all-pervasive spirit — must by reason of its universality have a nature common with our own, then we have solved the paradox of universal knowledge. We have realized our identity of being as at one with the Universal Mind, and the Universal Mind is the same as the Universal Law. Thus we arrive at the truth of St. John's statement, "Ye know all things," an intimate knowledge of the Universal Mind that exists and must remain on the spiritual plane.

This knowledge is to be found and experienced deep within as an intuitive "knowing." It is not of the realm of factual knowledge, and is therefore not something that we can state intellectually. Once we grasp it, however, in relating to the Universal Mind in order to manifest our desires, we can differentiate the undifferentiated (Universal Mind) in any direction that we choose. Our individual objective minds are able to divide the universal into parts, knowing that in reality the universe cannot be subdivided. We do so by embracing the aforementioned intuitive knowingness that what we wish to affect is part of us in that no separation exists between our objective mind and the Universal Mind.

Thus is recognition formed of the common identity of ourselves and the universal undifferentiated Spirit, which is the root and substance of all things. This releases us from the iron grasp of an inflexible Law. It does not do so by abrogating the Law, which would mean the annihilation of all things, but by producing in us an intelligence equal in affinity with the universal Law itself, and thus enabling us to apprehend and meet the requirements of the Law in each particular as it arises. In this way the Cosmic Intelligence becomes individualized, and the individual intelligence becomes universalized. The two become one, and in the proportion an individual realizes and acts upon this unity, it will be found that the Law, which gives rise to all outward conditions, whether of body or of circumstances, becomes more and more clearly understood, and can therefore be more freely made use of. By steady, intelligent endeavor to unfold upon these lines we may reach degrees of power to which it is impossible to assign any limits.

The student who would understand the rationale of the unfoldment of his own possibilities must make no mistake here. He must realize that the whole process is that of bringing the universal within the grasp of the individual by raising the individual to the level of the universal and not vice-versa. It is a mathematical truism that you cannot contract the infinite, and that you can expand the individual. It is precisely on these lines that evolution works. The laws of nature cannot be altered in the least degree, but we can come into such a realization of our own relation to the universal principle of Law that underlies them as to be able to press into our service all particular laws, whether of the visible or invisible side of Nature. In doing so, we find ourselves masters of the situation. This is to be accomplished by knowledge, and the only knowledge that will affect this purpose in all its countless immensity is the knowledge of the equivalency of our own personality and Universal Spirit.

Our recognition of this Spirit must therefore be twofold: 1.) as the principle of necessary sequence, order or Law, and 2.) as the principle of Intelligence, responsive to our own recognition of it.

VIII. RECIPROCAL ACTION OF THE UNIVERSAL AND INDIVIDUAL MINDS

THE foregoing considerations bring us to the border of theological speculation. Nevertheless, the student must bear in mind the Mental Scientist's business is to regard even the most exalted spiritual phenomena from a purely scientific standpoint. They are viewed as the workings of universal natural Law. If he thus simply deals with the facts as he finds them, little doubt can exist that the true meaning of many theological statements will come into focus.

It makes sense to adopt a rule that it is not necessary to have a theological explanation of a law in order to use it, either personally or impersonally. Therefore, the personal quality inherent in the universal underlying spirit that is present in all things cannot be too strongly insisted upon. We must remember that in dealing with it we are dealing with a purely natural power that reappears at every point in a fluid variety of forms, whether as person, animal, or thing. In each case, what it becomes to any individual is exactly measured by that individual's recognition of it. To each and all it bears the relation of supporter of the race, and where the individual development is incapable of realizing anything more, this is the limit of the relation. As the individual's power of recognition expands, he finds a reciprocal expansion on the part of this intelligent power that gradually develops into a consciousness of intimate companionship between an individualized mind and its unindividualized source.

Now, this is exactly the relation that on ordinary scientific principles we should expect to find between the individual and the cosmic mind. We do this on the supposition that the cosmic mind is subjective mind. For reasons already given, we can regard it in no other light. As subjective mind, it must reproduce exactly the conception of itself that the objective mind of the individual, acting through his own subjective mind, impresses upon it. At the same time, as creative mind, it builds up external facts in correspondence with this conception. *"Quot homines tot sententiae."* Each externalizes in his outward circumstances precisely his idea of the Universal Mind.

This is what the student must understand. A man can by the natural law of mind bring the Universal Mind into perfectly coordinated action with its own will. On the one hand, he can make it a source of infinite instruction, and on the other, a source of infinite power. He will thus wisely alternate the personal and impersonal aspects respectively between his individual mind and the Universal Mind. When he seeks guidance or strength, he will regard his own mind as the impersonal element that is to receive personality from the superior wisdom and force of the Greater Mind. On the other hand, when the time comes to give out the accumulated stores, he must reverse the position and consider his own mind as the personal element, and the Universal Mind as the impersonal. He can then direct the Universal Mind with certainty by impressing his own personal desire upon it.

We need not be staggered at the greatness of this conclusion, for it stems from the natural relationship between the subjective and the objective minds. The only question is whether we will limit our view to the lower level of the latter, or expand it to include the limitless possibilities that the subjective mind presents us.

I have dealt with this question at some length because it provides the key to two important subjects, the Law of Supply and the nature of Intuition. Students often find it easier to understand how a mind can influence another body other than its own, than how it can influence circumstances.

The answer is that the operation of thought-power is not confined to the individual mind. If one lesson exists that the student of Mental Science should take to heart more than another, it is that the action of thought-power is not limited to a particular individuality. In practicing thought-power, the individual gives direction to something that is unlimited, calling into action a force infinitely greater than his own. This force is in itself impersonal though intelligent, and as such will receive the impression of his personality. Therefore, it can make its influence felt far beyond the limits that surround the individual's objective perception of the circumstances with which he has to deal.

It is for this reason that I lay so much stress on the combination of two apparent opposites in the Universal Mind, the union of intelligence with impersonality. The intelligence not only enables it to receive the impression of our thought, but also causes it to devise exactly the right means for bringing it into accomplishment. This is only the logical result of the hypothesis that we are dealing with infinite Intelligence that is also synonymous with infinite Life. Life means Power, and infinite life therefore means limitless power. Limitless power moved by limitless intelligence cannot be conceived of as ever stopping short of the accomplishment of its object. Therefore, given the intention on the part of the Universal Mind, there can be no doubt as to its ultimate accomplishment.

Then comes the question of intention. How do we know what the intention of the Universal Mind may be? This raises the question of impersonality.

The answer is that it has no intention because it is impersonal. As I have already said, the Universal mind works by a law of averages for the advancement of the race. It is in no way concerned with the particular wishes of an individual. If his wishes are in line with the forward movement of the everlasting principle, there is nowhere in Nature any power to restrict him in their fulfillment. If they are opposed to the general forward movement, then they will bring him into collision with it, and the Universal mind will crush him. From the relation between the Universal mind and the individual mind, the same principle that shows itself in the individual mind as Will can be described in the Universal mind as a Law of Tendency. The direction of this tendency must always be to life-givingness because the universal mind is the undifferentiated Life-spirit of the universe. Therefore, in every case, the test is whether our particular intention is in this same lifeward direction. If it is, then we may be absolutely certain that there is no intention on the part of the Universal Mind to thwart the intention of our own individual mind.

We are dealing with a purely impersonal force that will no more oppose us by specific plans of its own than will steam or electricity. Combining, then, the Universal Mind's utter impersonality and its perfect intelligence, we find precisely the sort of natural force we would like to have working for us, a force that will undertake whatever we put into its hands without asking questions or bargaining for terms. And having undertaken our business, it will bring to bear an intelligence that makes the combined knowledge of the entire human race look like nothing. Along with this, it will bring power equal to this intelligence.

I may be using a rough and ready mode of expression, but my objective is to bring home to the student the nature of the power he can employ and the method of employing it. I may therefore state the whole position in this way: Your objective is not to run the whole cosmos, but rather to draw particular benefits, physical, mental, moral, or financial into your own or someone else's life. From this individual point of view the universal creative power has no mind of its own. Therefore you can make up its mind for it. When its mind is thus made up for it, it never vacates its place as the creative power. It at once sets to work to carry out the purpose for which it has thus been concentrated. Unless this concentration is dissipated by the same agency (yourself) that first produced it, it will work on by the law of growth to complete manifestation on the outward plane.

In dealing with this great impersonal intelligence, we are dealing with the infinite, and we must fully realize infinitude as that which touches all points. Since it does, there should be no difficulty in understanding that this intelligence can draw together the means requisite for its purpose even from the ends of the world. Understanding the Law in this way as we do, we must put aside all questioning as to the specific means which will be employed in any case. To question this is to sow a seed of doubt, and our first objective is to eradicate doubt. Our intellectual endeavor should therefore not be to attempt to foretell the various secondary causes that will eventually combine to produce the desired result, laying down beforehand what particular causes should be necessary, and from where they should come. Rather, we should direct our intellectual endeavor to seeing more clearly the rationale of the general law by which trains of secondary causes are set in motion.

Employed in the former way our intellect becomes the greatest hindrance to our success. It only helps to increase our doubts because it is trying to grasp particulars that are entirely outside its circle of vision. Employed in the latter, it affords the most material aid in maintaining that nucleus without which there is no center from which the principle of growth can assert itself. The intellect can only deduce consequences from facts that it is able to state. Consequently, it cannot deduce any assurance from facts of whose existence it cannot yet have any knowledge through the medium of the physical senses. For the same reason, it can realize the existence of a Law by which the as yet unmanifested circumstances may be brought into manifestation. Thus used in its right order, the intellect becomes the handmaid of that more interior power within us that manipulates the unseen substance of all things, and which we may call relative first cause.

IX. CAUSES AND CONDITIONS

THE expression "relative first cause" was used in the last section to distinguish the action of the creative principle in the individual mind from that of Universal First Cause, on the one hand, and from secondary causes on the other. Primary causation, as it exists in us, is the power to initiate a train of causation directed to a particular purpose. As the power of initiating a fresh sequence of cause and effect, it is first cause, and as referring to an individual purpose, it is relative. It may therefore be spoken of as relative first cause, or the power of primary causation manifested by the individual.

The understanding and use of this power is the whole object of Mental Science. It is necessary, therefore, that the student should clearly see the relation between causes and conditions. A simple illustration will go further for this purpose than any elaborate explanation.

If a lighted candle is brought into a room, the room becomes illuminated. If the candle is taken away, it becomes dark again. The illumination and the darkness are both conditions. One is positive resulting from the presence of the light. The other is negative resulting from its absence. From this simple example we see, therefore, that every positive condition has an exactly opposite negative condition corresponding to it. This correspondence results from their being related to the same cause, one positive and the other negative. Hence, we may lay down the rule that all positive conditions result from the active presence of a certain cause, and that all negative conditions from the absence of such a cause. A condition, whether positive or negative, is never primary cause. Moreover, the primary cause of any series can never be negative. To be negative is the condition that arises from the absence of an active cause. This should be thoroughly understood as it is the philosophical basis of all those "denials" that play so important a part in Mental Science, and that may be summed up in the statement that evil being negative, or the absence of good, has no substantive existence in itself.

Conditions whether positive or negative are no sooner called into existence than they become causes in their turn and produce further conditions, and so on ad infinitum. Thus they give rise to the whole train of secondary causes. So long as we judge only from the information conveyed to us by the outward senses, we are working on the plane of secondary causation and see nothing but a succession of conditions forming part of an endless train of antecedent conditions that come out of the past and stretch into the future. From this point of view, we are under the rule of an iron destiny from which there seems no possibility of escape. This is because the outward senses are only capable of dealing with the relations that one manner of limitation bears to another because the senses are no more than instruments by which the relative and the conditioned are made known to us.

The only way of escaping the iron destiny mentioned above is to rise out of the region of secondary causes into that of primary causation. Here is to be found the originating energy before it has passed into manifestation as a condition. This region is to be found within ourselves. It is the region of pure ideas. For this reason, I have laid stress on the two aspects of spirit as being pure thought and manifested form. The thought-image or ideal pattern of a thing is first cause relative to that thing. It is the substance of that thing unimpeded by any antecedent condition.

If we realize that all visible things must have their origin in spirit, then the whole creation around us is the standing evidence that the starting-point of all things is in thought-images or ideas. No other action of spirit than the formation of such images can be conceived of prior to an image's manifestation in matter. If, then, this is spirit's *modus operandi* for self-expression, we have only to transfer this conception from the scale of cosmic spirit working on the plane of the universal to that of individualized spirit working on the plane of the particular in order to see that the formation of an ideal image by means of our thought sets first cause in motion with regard to the specific object. No difference in kind exists between the operation of first cause in the universal and in the particular. The difference is only a difference of scale; the power itself identical. We must therefore always be clear as to whether we are consciously using first cause or not.

Note the word "consciously" because, whether consciously or unconsciously, we are always using first cause. It was for this reason that I emphasized the fact that the Universal Mind is purely subjective and therefore bound by the laws that apply to subjective mind on whatever scale. Hence we are always impressing some sort of ideas upon it, whether we are aware of the fact or not. All our existing limitations result from our having habitually impressed upon it that idea of limitation that we have acquired by restricting all possibility to the region of secondary causes. Investigation has shown us, however, that conditions are never causes in themselves. Rather, they are only the subsequent links of a chain started on the plane of the pure ideal. What we have to do is to reverse our method of thinking and regard the ideal as the real and the outward manifestation as a mere reflection. This reflection must change with every change of the objective that casts it. For these reasons, it is essential to know whether we are consciously making use of first cause with a definite purpose or not.

Here is how we can know. If we regard the fulfillment of our purpose as contingent upon any circumstances, past, present, or future, we are not making use of first cause. Rather, we have descended to the level of secondary causation, which is the region of doubts, fears, and limitations, all of which we are impressing upon the universal subjective mind with the inevitable result that it will build up corresponding external conditions. But if we realize that the region of secondary causes is the region of mere reflections, we shall not think of our purpose as contingent upon any conditions whatever. We shall know that by forming the idea of what we want in the absolute, and maintaining that idea, we have shaped the first cause into the desired form and can await the result with cheerful expectancy.

It is here that we find the importance of realizing spirit's independence of time and space. An ideal, as such, cannot be formed in the future. It must either be formed here and now or not be formed at all. It is for this reason that every teacher who has ever spoken with due knowledge of the subject has impressed upon his followers the necessity of picturing the fulfillment of their desires as already accomplished on the spiritual plane. This is the indispensable condition of fulfillment in the visible and concrete.

When this is properly understood, any anxious thought as

to the means to be employed in the accomplishment of our purposes is seen to be quite unnecessary. If the end is already secured, then it follows that all the steps leading to it are secured also. The means will pass into the smaller circle of our conscious activities day by day in due order. Then we have to work upon them, not with fear, doubt, or feverish excitement, but calmly and joyously, because we know that the end is already secured. The tasks and means we have before us represent only one portion of a much larger coordinated movement, the final result of which admits of no doubt.

Mental Science does not offer a premium to idleness, but it takes all work out of the region of anxiety and toil by assuring the worker of the success of his labor, if not in the precise form he anticipated, then in some other still better suited to his requirements. But suppose, when we reach a point where some momentous decision has to be made, we happen to decide wrongly? On the hypothesis that the end is already secured you cannot decide wrongly. Your right decision is as much one of the necessary steps in the accomplishment of the end as any of the other conditions leading up to it. Therefore, while being careful to avoid rash action, we may make sure that the same Law that is controlling the rest of the circumstances in the right direction will influence our judgment in that direction also.

To get good results we must properly understand our relation to the great impersonal power we are using. It is intelligent and we are intelligent, and the two intelligences must cooperate. We must not fly in the face of the Law by expecting it to do for us what it can only do through us, and we must therefore use our intelligence with the knowledge that it is acting as the instrument of a greater intelligence. Because we have this knowledge, we may and should cease from all anxiety as to the final result.

In actual practice we must first form the ideal conception of our objective with the definite intention of impressing it upon the Universal Mind. It is this intention that takes such thought out of the region of mere casual fancies. Then we must affirm that our knowledge of the Law is sufficient reason to hold a calm expectation of a corresponding result. Since all necessary conditions will come to us in due order, we can then turn to the affairs of daily life with the assurance that the initial conditions are either there already or will soon come into view. If we do not yet see them, let us rest in the knowledge that the spiritual prototype already exists and wait until some circumstance pointing in the desired direction begins to show itself.

This may be a very small circumstance, but it is the direction and not the magnitude that is to be taken into consideration. As soon as we see it, we should regard it as the first sprouting of the seed we have sown in the Absolute, and do calmly, and without excitement, whatever the circumstances may seem to require. Later on we shall see that doing this will in turn lead to further circumstances in the same direction until we find ourselves conducted step by step to the accomplishment of our objective. In this way the understanding of the great principle of the Law of Supply will, by repeated experiences, deliver us more and more completely out of the region of anxious thought and toilsome labor and bring us into a new world where the useful employment of all our powers, whether mental or physical, will only be an unfolding of our individuality upon the lines of its own nature, and therefore a perpetual source of health and happiness. This is a sufficient inducement, surely, to the careful study of the laws governing the relation between the individual and the Universal Mind.

X. INTUITION

WE have seen that the subjective mind is open to suggestion by the objective mind. But there is also an action of the subjective mind upon the objective. The individual's subjective mind is his own innermost self, and its first care is the maintenance of the individuality of which it is the foundation. Since it is pure spirit it has its continual existence in that plane of being where all things exist in the universal here and the everlasting now. Consequently, it can inform the lower mind of things removed from its range of sight either because of distance or because they are in the future.

The absence of the conditions of time and space must logically concentrate all things into a present focus. Therefore, we can assign no limit to the subjective mind's power of perception. Naturally, the question arises, why does it not keep the objective mind continually informed on all points? The answer is that it would do so if the objective mind were sufficiently trained to recognize the indications given. To supply this training is one of the purposes of Mental Science.

Once we recognize the position of the subjective mind as the supporter of the whole individuality, we cannot doubt that much of what we take to be the spontaneous movement of the objective mind has its origin in the subjective mind prompting the objective mind in the right direction without our conscious awareness. At times, when the urgency of the case seems to demand it, or when for some reason yet unknown the objective mind is for a while more closely en rapport with the subjective mind, the interior voice is heard strongly and persistently. When this is the case, we would do well to pay attention. Lack of space prevents me from giving examples, but no doubt the reader has had his own experience of this phenomenon.

The importance of understanding and following intuition cannot be exaggerated. Nevertheless, I candidly admit that it is difficult to maintain a happy median between total disregard of intuition and allowing ourselves to go overboard chasing daydreams. The best guide is the knowledge that comes of personal experience. This gradually leads to an inward sense of touch or feel that enables us to distinguish the true from the false. This appears to grow with the sincere desire for truth and with the recognition of the spirit as its source. One general principle the writer can deduce from his own experience is that the intuitive faculty is aware of facts that are unknowable by the objective mind at a given point of time. Another principle is that our very first impression of feeling on any subject is generally correct. Before the objective mind has begun to argue on the subject it is like the surface of a smooth lake which clearly reflects the light from above. As soon as it begins to argue because of outward appearances, however, these also throw their reflections upon its surface so that the original image becomes blurred and is no longer recognizable. Thus this first conception is quickly lost.

The first impression should, therefore, be carefully observed and registered in the memory with a view to testing the various arguments that subsequently will arise on the objective plane. It is, however, impossible to reduce so interior an action as that of intuition to the form of hard and fast rules. Beyond carefully noting particular cases as they occur, probably the best plan for the student will be to include the whole subject of intuition in the general principle of the Law of Attraction, especially if he sees how this law interacts with that personal quality of universal spirit of which we have already spoken.

XI. HEALING

THE subject of healing has been elaborately treated by many writers and fully deserves all the attention that has been given to it. Nevertheless, the objective of these lectures is to ground the student in those general principles on which all conscious use of the creative power of thought is based. It is not to lay down formal rules for all the specific applications of it. I will therefore examine the broad principles that appear to be common to the various methods of mental healing that are in use, each of which derives its efficacy, not from the peculiarity of the method, but from it being a method that allows the higher laws of Nature to come into play.

The principle universally laid down by all mental healers, in whatever various terms they may explain it, is that the basis of all healing is a change in belief. The sequence from which this results is as follows: the subjective mind is the creative faculty within us. It creates whatever the objective mind impresses upon it. The objective mind, or intellect, impresses its thought upon the subjective mind. The thought is the expression of the belief. Hence whatever the subjective mind creates is the reproduction externally of our beliefs.

Accordingly, in order to heal our goal must be to change our beliefs. We cannot do this, however, without some solid ground of conviction of the error of our old beliefs and of the truth of our new ones. This ground we find in that law of causation that I have endeavored to explain. The wrong belief that externalizes as sickness is the belief that some secondary cause, which is really only a condition, is a primary cause. The knowledge of the law shows that there is only one primary cause, and this is the factor in our own individuality that we call subjective or subconscious mind.

For this reason I have insisted on the difference between placing an idea in the subconscious mind, that is, on the plane of the absolute where no reference to time and space exists, and placing the same idea in the conscious intellectual mind that only perceives things as related to time and space. Now the only conception you can have of yourself in the absolute, or unconditioned, is as purely living Spirit, not hampered by conditions of any sort, and therefore not subject to illness. When this idea is firmly impressed on the subconscious mind, the subconscious mind will externalize it. The reason why this process is not always successful at the first attempt is that all our life we have been holding the false belief in sickness as a substantial entity in itself and a primary cause, instead of being merely a negative condition resulting from the absence of a primary cause. A belief that has become ingrained from childhood cannot be eradicated at a moment's notice.

We often find, therefore, that for some time after a treatment an improvement is seen in the patient's health. Then the old symptoms return. This is because the new belief in his own creative faculty has not yet had time to penetrate down to the innermost depths of the subconscious mind. Rather, it has only partially entered it. Each succeeding treatment strengthens the subconscious mind in its hold of the new belief until at last a permanent cure is affected. This is the method of self-treatment based on the patient's own knowledge of the law of his being.

But "there is not in all men this knowledge," or at any rate not such a full recognition of it as will enable them to give successful treatment to themselves. In these cases the intervention of the healer becomes necessary. The only difference between the healer and the patient is that the healer has learned how to control the less self-conscious modes of the spirit by the more self-conscious mode, while the patient has not yet attained this knowledge. What the healer does is to substitute his own objective or conscious mentality, which is will joined to intellect, for that of the patient, and in this way to find entrance to his subconscious mind and impress upon it the suggestion of perfect health.

The question then arises, how can the healer substitute his own conscious mind for that of the patient?

The answer shows the practical application of those very abstract principles that I have laid down in the earlier sections. Our ordinary conception of ourselves is that of an individual personality that ends where another personality begins. In other words, our thinking is that the two personalities are entirely separate. This is incorrect. There is no such hard and fast line of demarcation between personalities. The boundaries between one and another can be increased or reduced in rigidity according to will. In fact they may be temporarily removed so completely that, for the time being, the two personalities become merged into one.

The action that takes place between healer and patient depends on this principle. The patient is asked by the healer to put himself in a receptive mental attitude. This means that he is to exercise his volition for the purpose of removing the barrier of his own objective personality and thus affording entrance to the mental power of the healer. The healer does the same, only with this difference: while the patient withdraws the barrier on his side with the intention of admitting a flowing-in, the healer does so with the intention of allowing a flowing-out. Thus by the joint action of the two minds the barriers of both personalities are removed and the direction of the flow of volition is determined. It flows from the healer, as actively willing to give, towards the patient, as passively willing to receive. According to the universal law of Nature, the flow must always be to the vacuum from the space that is full.

This mutual removal of the external mental barrier between healer and patient is what is termed establishing a rapport between them. Here we find a most valuable practical application of the principle laid down earlier in this book — that pure spirit is present in its entirety at every point simultaneously. It is for this reason that as soon as the healer realizes that the barriers of external personality between himself and his patient have been removed, he can then speak to the subconscious mind of the patient as though it were his own. Since both are pure spirit, the thought of their identity makes them identical, and both are concentrated into a single entity at a single point upon which the conscious mind of the healer can be brought to bear according to the universal principle of the control of the subjective mind by the objective mind through suggestion. This is why I have insisted on the distinction between pure spirit, or spirit conceived of apart from extension in any matrix and the conception of it as so extended.

It should be duly noted that if we concentrate our mind upon the diseased condition of the patient, we are thinking of him as a separate personality, and are not fixing our mind upon that conception of him as pure spirit that in effect will give us entry to his springs of being. We must, therefore, not think about symptoms. Indeed we must not think about his corporeal personality. We must think of him as a purely spiritual individuality, and as such entirely free from the victimization of any conditions. Consequently, we will think of him as voluntarily externalizing the conditions most expressive of the vitality and intelligence so characteristic of pure spirit. Thinking of him thus, we then make mental affirmation that he shall build up outwardly the correspondence of that perfect vitality that he inwardly knows himself to be. This suggestion being impressed by the healer's conscious thought, while the patient's conscious thought is at the same time impressing the fact that he is receiving the active thought of the healer leads results in the patient's subconscious mind becoming thoroughly imbued with the recognition of its own life-giving power. According to the recognized law of subjective mentality, the patient's subconscious mind then proceeds to work out this suggestion into external manifestation, and thus is health substituted for sickness.

It must be understood that the purpose of the process here described is to strengthen the subject's individuality, not to dominate it. To use it for domination is inversion, bringing its appropriate penalty to the operator.

In this description I have contemplated the case where the patient is consciously cooperating with the healer, and it is in order to obtain this cooperation that the mental healer usually makes a point of instructing the patient in the broad principles of Mental Science, if he is not already acquainted with them. But this is not always advisable or possible. If they are opposed to prejudices and ideas held by the patient, the statement of principles may actually arouse his opposition.

Any active antagonism on the patient's part must tend to intensify the barrier of conscious personality which it is the healer's first objective to remove. In these cases nothing is so effective as absent treatment.

If the student has grasped all that has been said on the subject of spirit and matter, he will see that in mental treatment time and space count for nothing because the whole action takes place on a plane where these conditions do not exist. It is therefore quite immaterial whether the patient is in the immediate presence of the healer or in a distant country. Under these circumstances it is found through experience that one of the most effectual manners of mental healing is by treatment during sleep. Then the patient's entire system is in a natural state of relaxation. This prevents him offering any conscious opposition to the treatment.

By the same rule, the healer also is able to treat even more effectively during his own sleep than while waking. Before going to sleep he firmly impresses on his subjective mind that it is to convey a curative suggestion to the subjective mind of the patient, and then, by the general principles of the relation between subjective and objective mind, this suggestion is carried out during all the hours that the conscious individuality is wrapped in repose. This method is applicable to young children to whom the principles of the science cannot be explained. This method also can work on persons at a distance. Indeed the only advantage gained by the personal meeting of the patient and healer is in the instruction that can be orally given, or when the patient is at that early stage of knowledge where the healer's visible presence conveys the suggestion that something is then being done which could not be done in his absence. Otherwise, the presence or absence of the patient does not matter. The student must always remember that the subconscious mind does not have to work through the intellect or conscious mind to produce its curative effects. It is part of the all-pervading creative force of Nature, while the intellect is not creative but distributive.

From mental healing it is but a step to telepathy, clairvoyance and other kindred manifestations of transcendental power that are from time to time exhibited by the subjective entity and that follow laws as accurate as those that govern what we are accustomed to consider our more normal faculties. But these subjects do not properly fall within the scope of a book whose purpose is to lay down the broad principles that underlie all spiritual phenomena. Until these are clearly understood, the student cannot profitably attempt the detailed study of the more interior powers. To do so without a firm foundation of knowledge, and some experience in its practical application, would only be to expose himself to unknown dangers. This would be contrary to the scientific principle that the advance into the unknown can only be made from the standpoint of the known. If we do otherwise, we travel into a confused region of guesswork without any clearly defined principles for our guidance.

XII. THE WILL

THE Will is of such primary importance that the student should be on his guard against any mistake as to the position it holds in the mental economy. Many writers and teachers insist on willpower as though that were the creative faculty. No doubt intense willpower can evolve certain external results, but like all other methods of compulsion it lacks the permanency of natural growth. The appearances, forms, and conditions produced by mere intensity of willpower will only hang together so long as the compelling force continues. But let willpower be exhausted or withdrawn and the elements thus forced into unnatural combination will at once revert to their natural relationships. This is because the form created by compulsion did not have the germ of vitality in itself. It is therefore dissipated as soon as the external energy which supported it is withdrawn.

The mistake made by those who put much stock in willpower is in attributing the creative power to the will. Or, perhaps I should say that the mistake is in attributing the creative power to ourselves at all. The truth is that man never creates anything. His function is not to create, but rather to combine and distribute that which already exists. What we call our creations are new combinations of already existing material, whether mental or physical. This is amply demonstrated in the physical sciences. No one speaks of creating energy, but only of transforming one form of energy into another. If we realize this as a universal principle, we shall see that on the mental plane as well as on the physical, we never create energy but only provide the conditions by which the energy already existing in one mode can exhibit itself in another. Therefore, what relative to man we call his creative power is in reality that receptive attitude of expectancy which, so to say, makes a mold into which the malleable and as yet undifferentiated substance can flow and take the desired form. The will has much the same place in our mental machinery that the tool-holder has on a power-lathe. Like the tool-holder, the will is not the power but it does keep the mental faculties in that position relative to the power that enables the power to do the desired work. If, using the word in its widest sense, we may say that the imagination is the creative function, we may call the will the centralizing principle. Its function is to keep the imagination centered in the right direction.

We are aiming at consciously controlling our mental powers instead of letting them hurry us hither and thither in a purposeless manner. We must therefore understand the relationship of these powers to each other for the production of external results. First the whole train of causation is started by some emotion that gives rise to a desire. Next the judgment determines whether we shall externalize this desire or not. Then, the desire having been approved by the judgment, the will comes forward and directs the imagination to form the necessary spiritual prototype. The imagination thus centered on a particular object creates the spiritual nucleus, which in its turn acts as a center around which the forces of attraction begin to work. These continue to operate until, by the law of growth, the concrete result becomes perceptible to our external senses.

The business of the will, then, is to retain the various faculties of our mind in that position where they are really doing the work we wish, and this position may be generalized into the three following attitudes: Either we wish to act upon something, or be acted on by it, or to maintain a neutral position. In other words we either intend to project a force, or receive a force, or keep a position of inactivity relative to some particular object. Judgment determines which of these three positions we shall take up — the consciously active, the consciously receptive, or the consciously neutral. Then the function of the will is simply to maintain the position we have determined upon.

If we maintain any given mental attitude, we may reckon with all certainty on the law of attraction drawing us to those correspondences that outwardly symbolize the attitude in question. This is very different from the semi-animal screwing-up of the nervous forces which, with some people, stands for willpower. It implies no strain on the nervous system and is consequently not followed by any sense of exhaustion. The willpower, when transferred from the region of the lower mentality to the spiritual plane, becomes simply a calm and peaceful determination to retain a certain mental attitude in spite of all temptations to the contrary, knowing that by doing so the desired result will certainly appear.

The training of the will and its transference from the lower to the higher plane of our nature are among the first objects of Mental Science. The man is summed up in his will. Whatever he does by his own will is his own act. Whatever he does without the consent of his will is not his own act but that of the power by which his will was coerced. But we must recognize that, on the mental plane, no other individuality can obtain control over our will unless we first allow it to do so. It is for this reason that all legitimate use of Mental Science is towards the strengthening of the will, whether in ourselves or others, and bringing it under the control of an enlightened reason.

When the will realizes its power to deal with first cause it is no longer necessary for the operator to state to himself all the philosophy of its action every time he wishes to use it. But knowing that the trained will is a tremendous spiritual force acting on the plane of first cause, he simply expresses his desire with the intention of operating on that plane and knows that the desire thus expressed will in due time externalize itself as concrete fact. He now sees that the point that really demands his earnest attention is not whether he possesses the power of externalizing any results he chooses, but rather, that of learning to choose wisely what results to produce. Let us not suppose that even the highest powers will take us out of the law of cause and effect. We can never set any cause in motion without calling forth those effects that it already contains in embryo and that will again become causes in their turn, thus producing a series that must continue to flow until it is cut short by bringing into operation a cause of an opposite character to the one that originated it. Thus we shall find the field for the exercise of our intelligence continually expanding with the expansion of our powers.

We may not be able to see very far, but there is one safe general principle to be gained from what has already been said about causes and conditions. This is that the whole sequence always partakes of the same character as the initial cause. If that character is negative, that is, destitute of any desire to externalize kindness, cheerfulness, strength, beauty or some other sort of good, this negative quality will make itself felt all down the line. But if the opposite affirmative character is in the original motive, then it will reproduce its kind in forms of love, joy, strength and beauty with unerring precision. Before setting out, therefore, to produce new conditions by the exercise of our thought-power we should weigh carefully what further results they are likely to lead to. Here, again, we shall find an ample field for the training of our will, in learning to acquire that self-control that will enable us to postpone an inferior present satisfaction in preference to a greater prospective good.

These considerations naturally lead us to the subject of concentration. I have just now pointed out that all duly controlled mental action consists in holding the mind in one of three attitudes. But there is a fourth mental condition, which is that of letting our mental functions run on without our will directing them to any definite purpose. It is on this word, "purpose," that we must fix our whole attention. Instead of dissipating our energies, we must follow an intelligent method of concentration. The word means being gathered up at a center, and the center of anything is that point in which all its forces are equally balanced. To concentrate, therefore, means first to bring our minds into a condition of equilibrium that will enable us to consciously direct the flow of spirit to a definitely recognized purpose, then carefully to guard our thoughts from inducing a flow in the opposite direction. We must always bear in mind that we are dealing with a wonderful potential energy that is not yet differentiated into any particular mode, and that by the action of our mind we can differentiate it into any specific mode of activity that we will. By keeping our thought fixed on the fact that the inflow of this energy is taking place, and that by our mental attitude we are determining its direction, we shall gradually realize a corresponding externalization. Proper concentration, therefore, does not consist of strenuous effort that exhausts the nervous system and defeats its own objective by suggesting the consciousness of an adverse force to be fought against, thus creating the adverse circumstances we dread. Rather, it consists in shutting out all thoughts of a kind that would disperse the spiritual nucleus we are forming, and in dwelling cheerfully on the knowledge that, because the law is certain in its action, our desire is certain of accomplishment.

The other great principle to be remembered is that concentration is for the purpose of determining the quality we are going to give to the previously undifferentiated energy rather than to arrange the specific circumstances of its manifestation. That is the work of the creative energy itself, which will build up its own forms of expression quite naturally if we allow it, thus saving us a great deal of needless anxiety. What we really want is expansion in a certain direction, whether of health, wealth, or what not. So long as we get this, what does it matter whether it reaches us through some channel that we thought we could reckon upon or through some other whose existence we had not suspected. It is the fact that we are concentrating energy of a particular kind for a particular purpose that we should fix our minds upon, and not look upon any specific details as essential to the accomplishment of our object.

These are the two golden rules regarding concentration. But we must not suppose that because we have to be on our guard against idle drifting there is to be no such thing as repose. On the contrary, it is during periods of repose that we accumulate strength for action

Repose does not mean a state of purposelessness. As pure spirit the subjective mind never rests. It is only the objective mind in its connection with the physical body that needs rest. Though there are no doubt times when the greatest possible rest is to be obtained by stopping the action of our conscious thought altogether, the more generally advisable method is by changing the direction of the thought and, instead of centering it upon something we intend to do, letting it dwell quietly upon what we are. This direction of thought might, of course, develop into the deepest philosophical speculation, but it is not necessary that we should be always either consciously projecting our forces to produce some external effect or working out the details of some metaphysical problem. We may simply realize ourselves as part of the universal Life and thus gain a quiet centralization, which, though maintained by a conscious act of the will, is the very essence of rest. From this standpoint we see that all is Life and all is Good, and that Nature, from her clearly visible surface to her most arcane depths, is one vast storehouse of life and good entirely devoted to our individual use. We have the key to all her treasures, and we can now apply our knowledge of the law of being without entering into all those details that are only needed for purposes of study. In doing so we find it results in our having acquired the consciousness of our oneness with the whole. This is the great secret. When we have once fathomed it, we can enjoy our possession of the whole, or of any part of it, because by our recognition we have made it our own and can increasingly make it so.

Whatever most appeals to us at any particular time or place is that mode of the universal living spirit with which we are most in touch at that moment. Realizing this, we shall draw from it streams of vital energy that will make the very sensation of living a joy. We will radiate a sphere of vibration from us that can deflect all injurious suggestion on whatever plane. We may not have literary, artistic, or scientific skill that we can employ in order to present to others the results of our communings with Nature, but the joy of this sympathetic indrawing will nevertheless produce a corresponding outflow manifesting itself in the happier look and kindlier demeanor of a person who thus realizes his oneness with every aspect of the whole. He realizes, and this is the great point, in that attitude of mind that is not directed to any specific external object that, for himself, he is and always must be the center of all this galaxy of Life. Thus he contemplates himself as seated at the center of infinity, not an infinity of blank space, but rather one pulsating with Life, in all of which he knows that the true essence is nothing but good. This is the very opposite of being selfishly self-centered. It is the center where we find that we both receive from all and flow out to all. Apart from this principle of circulation there is no true life, and if we contemplate our central position only as affording us greater advantages for in-taking, we have missed the whole point of our studies by missing the real nature of the Life-principle, which is action and reaction. If we would have life enter into us, we ourselves must enter into life — enter into the spirit of it, just as we must enter into the spirit of a book or a game to enjoy it.

There can be no action at a center only. There must be a perpetual flowing out towards the circumference, and then back again to the center to maintain a vital activity. Otherwise collapse must ensue either from anemia or congestion. But if we realize the reciprocal nature of the vital pulsation, and that the out-flowing consists in the habit of mind that gives itself to the good it sees in others, rather than in any specific actions, then we shall find that the cultivation of this disposition will provide innumerable avenues for the universal life force to flow through us, whether as giving or receiving. This we had never before suspected. This action and reaction will so build up our own vitality that each day will find us more thoroughly alive than any that had preceded it. This, then, is the attitude of repose in which we may enjoy all the beauties of science, literature and art or may peacefully commune with the spirit of nature without the aid of any third mind to act as its interpreter. This is still a purposeful attitude although not directed to a specific object. We have not allowed the will to relax its control, but have merely altered its direction. For in action and repose alike we find that our strength lies in our recognition of the unity of the spirit and of ourselves as individual concentrations of it.

XIII. IN TOUCH WITH SUBCONSCIOUS MIND

THE preceding pages have made the student aware in some measure of the immense importance of our dealings with the subconscious mind. Our relation to it, whether on the scale of the individual or the universal, is the key to all that we are or ever can be. In its unrecognized working, it is the spring of all that we can call the automatic action of mind and body. On the universal scale it is the silent power of evolution gradually working onwards to that "divine event, to which the whole creation moves," and by our conscious recognition of it we make it, relative to ourselves, all that we believe it to be. The closer our rapport with it becomes, the more of what in the past we have considered automatic action, whether in our bodies or our circumstances, will pass under our control. Eventually, we shall control our whole individual world.

Since, then, this is the stupendous issue involved, the question of how we are to put ourselves practically in touch with the subconscious mind is a very important one. The clue that gives us direction can be found in the impersonal quality of subconscious mind. It is not impersonal in that it lacks the elements of personality. The individual subjective mind is not impersonal in that it lacks a sense of individuality. It is impersonal in that it does not recognize relationships outside itself such as happy and sad, serious or lighthearted that to the objective mind constitute its personality.

If we would become in touch with the subconscious mind we must meet it on its own ground. It can see things only from the deductive standpoint. Therefore it cannot take note of the inductive standpoint from which we construct the idea of our external personality. Accordingly, we cannot put ourselves in touch with it by bringing it down to the level of the external and nonessential. We can get in touch only by rising to its level on the plane of the interior and essential.

How can this be done? Let two well-known writers answer.

Rudyard Kipling tells us in his story of Kim how the boy at times would lose his sense of personality by repeating to himself the question, "Who is Kim?" Gradually his personality would seem to fade and he would experience a feeling of passing into a grander and a wider life in which the boy, Kim, was unknown. His own conscious individuality remained, but was exalted and expanded to an inconceivable extent

In Tennyson's life written by his son we are told that at times the poet had a similar experience.

The message is that we come into touch with the absolute exactly in proportion that we withdraw ourselves from the relative. They vary inversely to each other.

For the purpose, then, of getting in touch with our subconscious mind we must endeavor to think of ourselves as pure being, as the interior entity that supports our outward manifestation. In doing so we shall realize that the essential quality of pure being must be good. It is in itself pure Life and as such cannot desire anything detrimental to pure Life in whatever form it has manifested. Consequently, the purer our intentions, the more readily we shall place ourselves *en rapport* with our subjective entity. Fortunately, the same applies to that Greater Subconscious Mind of which our individual subjective mind is a particular manifestation. In actual practice the process consists in first forming a clear conception in the objective mind of the idea we wish to convey to the subjective mind. Then, when this has been firmly grasped, our endeavor should be to lose sight of all other facts connected with the external personality except the one in question, and then mentally address the subjective mind as though it were an independent entity and impress upon it what you want it to do or to believe.

Everyone must formulate his own way of working, but one method, both simple and effective, is to say to the subjective mind, "This is what I want you to do. You will now step into my place and do it, bringing all your powers and intelligence to bear, and considering yourself to be none other than myself."

Having done this, you can return to the realization of your own objective personality and leave the subjective mind to perform its task in full confidence that, by the law of its nature, it will do so if not hindered by a repetition of contrary messages from the objective mind. This is not mere fancy but a truth daily proved by the experience of increasing numbers. The facts have not been fabricated to fit the theory. The theory has been built up by careful observation of the facts.

Since it has been shown both by theory and practice that such is the law of the relation between subjective and objective mind, we find ourselves face to face with a very momentous question. Is there any reason why the laws that hold true with respect to the individual subjective mind should not hold be true of the Universal Mind as well?

The answer is that there is not.

As has been already shown the Universal Mind must, by its very universality, be purely subjective, and what is the law of a part must also be the law of the whole. The qualities of fire are the same whether the centers of combustion are great or small. Therefore we may well conclude these lectures by considering what will be the result if we apply what we have learned regarding the individual subjective mind to the Universal Mind.

We have learned that the three great facts regarding subjective mind are its creative power, its amenability to suggestion, and its inability to work by any other than the deductive method. This last is an exceedingly important point, for it implies that the action of the subjective mind is in no way limited by precedent. The inductive method works on principles inferred from an already existing pattern, and therefore at the best only produces the old thing in a new shape. But the deductive method works according to the essence or spirit of the principle, and does not depend on any previous concrete manifestation for its apprehension of it. This latter method of working must necessarily be that of the all-originating Mind, for since there could be no prior existing pattern from which it could learn the principles of construction, the lack of a pattern would have prevented its creating anything had its method been inductive instead of deductive. Thus by necessity, the Universal Mind must act deductively, that is, according to the law which has been found true of the individual subjective mind. It is thus not bound by any precedent. This means that its creative power is absolutely unlimited. Since it is essentially subjective mind, and not objective mind, it is entirely open to suggestion.

Whether in the individual or the universal, an unavoidable inference from the identity of the law governing subjective mind is this. Just as we can by suggestion impress a certain character of personality upon the individual subjective mind, so we can, and do, upon the Universal Mind. It is for this reason that I have drawn attention to the inherent personal quality of pure spirit when contemplated in its most interior plane.

The most important of all considerations, therefore, is with what character we invest the Universal Mind. Since our relation to it is purely subjective it will infallibly bear to us exactly that character which we impress upon it. In other words, it will be to us exactly what we believe it to be. This is simply a logical inference from the fact that, as subjective mind, our primary relation to it can only be on the subjective plane, and indirectly our objective relations must also spring from the same source. This is the meaning of that remarkable passage twice repeated in the Bible, "With the pure thou wilt show thyself pure, and with the crooked thou wilt show thyself perverse," (Ps. XVIII., 26, and II. Sam. XXII., 27, Revised Standard Version, Second Edition), for the context makes it clear that these words are addressed to the Divine Being.

The spiritual kingdom is within us, and as we realize it there so it becomes to us a reality. It is the unvarying law of the subjective life that "as a man thinketh in his heart so is he," that is to say, his inward subjective states are the only true reality, and what we call external realities are only their objective correspondences. If we thoroughly realize the truth that the Universal Mind must be to us exactly according to our conception of it, and that this relation is not merely imaginary but by the law of subjective mind must be to us an actual fact and the foundation of all other facts, then it is impossible to overestimate the importance of the conception of the Universal Mind that we adopt.

To the uninstructed there is little or no choice: they form a conception in accordance with the tradition they have received from others. Until they have learned to think for themselves, they have to abide by the results of that tradition. For natural laws admit of no exceptions, and however faulty the traditional idea may be, its acceptance will involve a corresponding reaction upon the Universal Mind. This will in turn be reflected into the conscious mind and external life of the individual. But those who understand the law of the subjective mind have no one but themselves to blame if they do not derive all possible benefits from it.

The greatest Teacher of Mental Science the world has ever seen has laid down sufficiently plain rules for our guidance. With a knowledge of the subject whose depth can be appreciated only by those who have themselves some practical acquaintance with it, He told the unlearned audiences who listened to him to regard the Universal Mind as a benign Father. He said to think of the Universal Mind as tenderly compassionate of all and sending the common bounties of Nature alike on the evil and the good. He also pictured It as exercising a special and individualized care over those who recognize Its willingness to do so, i.e. "the very hairs of your head are all numbered," and "ye are of more value than many sparrows."

Prayer was to be made to the unseen Being, not with doubt or fear, but with the absolute assurance of a certain answer. No limit was to be set to its power or willingness to work for us. But for those who did not understand this, the Great Mind was an adversary who cast them into prison until they paid the uttermost price. Thus in all cases the Master impressed upon his hearers the exact correspondence of the attitude of this unseen Power towards them with their own attitude towards it. Such teaching was not a narrow anthropomorphism but the adaptation to the intellectual capacity of the unlettered multitude of the very deepest truths of what we now call Mental Science. And the basis of it all is the cryptic personality of spirit hidden throughout the infinity of Nature under every form of manifestation.

As pure Life and Intelligence it can be no other than good. It can entertain no intention of evil. Thus all intentional evil must put us in opposition to it, and so deprive us of the consciousness of its guidance and strengthening and thus leave us to grope our own way and fight our own battle single-handed against the universe. Such odds will at last surely prove too great for us. But remember that the opposition can never be on the part of the Universal Mind, for it is in itself subconscious mind. To suppose any active opposition taken on its own initiative would be contrary to all we have learned as to the nature of subconscious mind whether in the individual or the universal. The position of the Universal Mind towards us is always the reflection of our own attitude. Therefore, although the Bible is full of threatening against those who persist in conscious opposition to the Divine Law of Good, it is on the other hand full of promises of immediate and full forgiveness to all who change their attitude and desire to cooperate with the Law of Good so far as they know it.

The laws of Nature do not act vindictively. Through all theological methods and traditional interpretations, let us realize that what we are dealing with is the supreme law of our own being. It is on the basis of this natural law that we find such declarations as that in Ezek. XVIII., 22, which tells that if we forsake our evil ways our past transgressions shall never again be mentioned to us.

We are dealing with the great principles of our subjective being, and our misuse of them in the past can never make them change their inherent law of action. If our method of using them in the past has brought us sorrow, fear and trouble, we have only to fall back on the law that if we reverse the cause, the effects will be reversed also. So what we have to do is simply to reverse our mental attitude and then endeavor to act up to the new one. The sincere endeavor to act up to our new mental attitude is essential, for we cannot really think in one way and act in another. But our repeated failures to fully act as we would wish must not discourage us. It is the sincere intention that is the essential thing, and this will in time release us from the bondage of habits that at present seem almost insurmountable.

The initial step, then, consists in determining to picture the Universal Mind as the ideal of all we could wish it to be, both to ourselves and to others. Additionally, we must endeavor to reproduce this ideal, however imperfectly, in our own life.

This step having been taken, we can then cheerfully look upon Universal Mind as our ever-present Friend, providing all good, guarding from all danger, and guiding us with all counsel. Gradually, as the habit of thus regarding the Universal Mind grows upon us, we shall find that in accord with the laws we have been considering, it will become more and more personal to us. In response to our desire its inherent intelligence will make itself more and more clearly perceptible to us as a power of perceiving truth far beyond any statement of truth that we could formulate by merely intellectual investigation. Similarly, if we think of it as a great power devoted to supplying all our needs, we shall imprint this character upon it, also. By the law of subjective mind it will take on the guardianship role we have credited it with playing.

If we would draw to ourselves some particular benefit beyond general care, the same rule holds good of impressing our desire upon the Universal Subjective Mind. If we realize that above and beyond all this we want something still greater and more enduring, the building-up of character and unfolding of our powers so that we may expand into fuller and yet fuller measures of joyous and joy-giving Life, the same rule still holds. We must simply convey to the Universal Mind the suggestion of the desire, and by the law of relation between subjective and objective mind this too will be fulfilled. Thus the deepest problems of philosophy bring us back to the old statement of the Law, "Ask and ye shall receive, seek and ye shall find, knock and it shall be opened unto you." This is the summing-up of the natural law of the relation between us and the Divine Mind.

It is no vain boast that Mental Science can enable us to make our lives what we will. We must start where we are now, and by rightly estimating our relation to the Divine Universal Mind we can gradually grow into any conditions we desire, provided we first make ourselves the person who corresponds to those conditions by adopting the appropriate mental attitude. For we can never get over the law of correspondence. The externalization will always be in accord with the internal principle that gives rise to it. To this law there is no limit. What it can do for us today it can do tomorrow, and through all that procession of tomorrows that loses itself in the dim vistas of eternity.

Belief in limitation is the one and only thing that causes limitation. This is because we thus impress limitation upon the creative principle. In proportion as we lay that belief aside our boundaries will expand, and increasing life and more abundant blessing will be ours.

But we must not ignore our responsibilities. Trained thought is far more powerful than untrained, and therefore the more deeply we penetrate into Mental Science the more carefully we must guard against all thoughts and words expressive of even the most modified form of ill-will. Gossip, talebearing, sneering laughter, are not in accord with the principles of Mental Science. Similarly, even our smallest thoughts of good carry with them a seed of good that will assuredly bear fruit in due time. This is not mere "goodie, goodie," but an important lesson in Mental Science, for our subjective mind takes its color from our settled mental habits, and an occasional affirmation or denial will not be sufficient to change it. We must therefore cultivate that tone which we wish to see reproduced in our conditions whether of body, mind, or circumstance.

In these lectures my purpose has been not so much to give specific rules of practice as to lay down the broad general principles of Mental Science. This will enable the student to form rules for himself. In every walk in life, book knowledge is only a means to an end. Books can only direct us where to look and what to look for. We must do the finding for ourselves. Therefore, if you have really grasped the principles of the science, you will frame rules of your own which will give you better results than any attempt to follow somebody else's method. Inevitably, this was successful in their hands precisely because it was theirs. Never fear to be yourself. If Mental Science does not teach you to be yourself, it teaches you nothing. Yourself, more yourself, and yet more yourself is what you want — only with the knowledge that the true self includes the inner and higher self that is always in immediate touch with the Great Divine Mind.

As Walt Whitman said, "You are not all included between your hat and your boots."

The growing popularity of the Edinburgh Lectures on Mental Science has led me to add to the present edition three more sections on Body, Soul, and Spirit, which it is hoped will prove useful by rendering the principles of the interaction of these three factors somewhat clearer.

XIV. THE BODY

SOME students find it difficult to realize that mental action can produce any real effect upon material substance. If this is not possible, there is no such thing as Mental Science, the purpose of which is to produce improved conditions both of body and environment so that the ultimate manifestation aimed at is always one of demonstration upon the plane of the visible and concrete. Therefore, to convince the student of an actual connection between the visible and the invisible, between the inner and the outer, is one of the most important undertakings in the course of our studies.

That such a connection must exist is proved by metaphysical argument in answer to the question, "How did anything ever come into existence at all?" The whole of creation, ourselves included, stands as evidence to this great truth. But to many minds merely abstract argument is not completely convincing, or at any rate it becomes more convincing if it is supported by something of a more concrete nature. For such readers I would give a few hints as to the correspondence between the physical and the mental. The subject covers a very wide area, and the limited space at my disposal will only allow me to touch on a few suggestive points. Still these may be sufficient to show that the abstract argument has some corresponding facts behind it.

One of the most convincing proofs I have seen is that afforded by the "biometre," a little instrument invented by an eminent French scientist, the late Dr. Hippolyte Baraduc, that shows the action of what he calls the "vital current." His theory is that this force, whatever its actual nature may be, is universally present, and operates as a current of physical vitality flowing perpetually with more or less energy through every physical organism. It is a force that can to some extent, at least, be controlled by the power of the human will. The theory in all its detail is exceedingly elaborate, and has been described in detail in Dr. Baraduc's published works. In a conversation I had with him about a year ago, he told me he was writing another book which would throw further light on the subject, but a few months later he passed over before it was presented to the world. The fact, however, that I wish to put before the reader is the ocular demonstration of the connection between mind and matter. This is an experiment that the biometre affords.

The instrument consists of a bell glass, from the inside of which is suspended a copper needle by a fine silken thread. The glass stands on a wooden support below which is a coil of copper wire. This, however, is not connected with any battery or other apparatus. It merely serves to condense the current. Below the needle, inside the glass, is a circular card divided into degrees to mark the action of the needle. Two of these instruments are placed side by side, but in no way are they connected. The experimenter then holds out the fingers of both hands to within about an inch of the glasses. According to the theory, the current enters at the left hand, circulates through the body, and passes out at the right hand. That is to say, an in-drawing occurs at the left and a giving-out at the right, thus agreeing with Reichenbach's experiments on the polarity of the human body.

I must confess that, although I had read Dr. Baraduc's

book, *Les Vibrations Humaines*, I approached the instrument in a very skeptical frame of mind. But I was soon convinced of my error. At first, holding a mental attitude of entire relaxation, I found that the left-hand needle was attracted through twenty degrees, while the right-hand needle, the one affected by the outgoing current, was repelled through ten degrees. After allowing the instrument to return to its normal equilibrium, I again approached it with the purpose of seeing whether a change of mental attitude would in the least modify the flow of current. This time I assumed the strongest mental attitude I could with the intention of sending out a flow through the right hand, and the result was remarkable compared with the previous one. The left-hand needle was now attracted only through ten degrees, while the right-hand one was deflected through something over thirty, thus clearly indicating the influence of the mental faculties in modifying the action of the current. I may mention that the experiment was made in the presence of two medical men who noted the movement of the needles.

I will not here stop to discuss the question of what the actual constitution of this current of vital energy may be — it is sufficient for our present purpose that it is there. The experiment I have described brings us face to face with the fact of a correspondence between our own mental attitude and the invisible forces of nature. Even if we say that this current is some form of electricity, and that the variation of its action is determined by changes in the polarization of the atoms of the body, then this change of polarity is the result of mental action. The quickening or retarding of the cosmic current is equally the result of the mental attitude whether we suppose our mental force to act directly upon the current itself or indirectly by inducing changes in the molecular structure of the body. Whichever hypothesis we adopt the conclusion is the same, namely, that the mind has power to open or close the door to invisible forces in such a way that the result of the mental action becomes apparent on the material plane.

Now, investigation shows that the physical body is a mechanism specially adapted for the transmutation of the inner or mental power into modes of external activity. We know from medical science that the whole body is traversed by a network of nerves which serve as the channels of communication between the indwelling, spiritual ego that we call mind, and the functions of the external organism. This nervous system is dual. One system, known as the Sympathetic, is the channel for all those activities which are not consciously directed by our will, such as the operation of the digestive organs, the repair of the daily wear and tear of the tissues, and the like. The other system, known as the Voluntary or Cerebrospinal system, is the channel through which we receive conscious perception from the physical senses and exercise control over the movements of the body. This system has its center in the brain, while the other has its center in a ganglionic mass at the back of the stomach known as the solar plexus, sometimes spoken of as the abdominal brain. The cerebrospinal system is the channel of our volitional or conscious mental action, and the sympathetic system is the channel of that mental action that unconsciously supports the vital functions of the body. Thus the cerebrospinal system is the organ of conscious mind and the sympathetic is that of subconscious mind.

But the interaction of conscious and subconscious mind requires a similar interaction between the corresponding systems of nerves. One conspicuous connection by which this is provided is the nerve. This nerve passes out of the cerebral region as a portion of the voluntary system. Through it we control the vocal organs. Then it passes onwards to the thorax sending out branches to the heart and lungs. Finally, it passes through the diaphragm, where it loses the outer coating that distinguishes the nerves of the voluntary system, and it becomes identified with those of the sympathetic system, so forming a connecting link between the two and making the man physically a single entity. Similarly, different areas of the brain indicate their connection with the objective and subjective activities of the mind respectively. Speaking in a general way, we may assign the frontal portion of the brain to the former and the posterior portion to the latter, while the intermediate portion partakes of the character of both.

The intuitional faculty has its correspondence in this upper area of the brain situated between the frontal and posterior portions. Physiologically speaking, it is here that intuitive ideas find entrance. These at first are more or less unformed and generalized in character, but are nevertheless perceived by the conscious mind. Otherwise we should not be aware of them at all. Then the effort of nature is to bring these ideas into more definite and usable shape, so the conscious mind lays hold of them and induces a corresponding vibratory current in the voluntary system of nerves, and this in turn induces a similar current in the involuntary system, thus handing the idea over to the subjective mind. The vibratory current which had first descended from the apex of the brain to the frontal brain and thus through the voluntary system to the solar plexus is now reversed and ascends from the solar plexus through the sympathetic system to the posterior brain, this return current indicating the action of the subjective mind.

If we were to remove the surface portion of the apex of the brain we should find immediately below it the shining belt of brain substance called the "corpus callosum." This is the point of union between the subjective and objective. As the current returns from the solar plexus to this point, it is restored to the objective portion of the brain in a fresh form that it has acquired by the silent alchemy of the subjective mind. Thus the conception, which was at first only vaguely recognized, is restored to the objective mind in a definite and workable form. Then the objective mind, acting through the frontal brain — the area of comparison and analysis — proceeds to work upon a clearly perceived idea and to bring out the potentialities latent in it.

It must of course be borne in mind that I am here speaking of the mental ego in that mode of its existence with which we are most familiar, that is as clothed in flesh, although there may be much to say as to other modes of its activity. But for our daily life we have to consider ourselves as we are in that aspect of life. From this point of view, the physiological correspondence of the body to the action of the mind is an important item. Therefore, although we must always remember that the origin of ideas is purely mental, we must not forget that on the physical plane every mental action implies a corresponding molecular action in the brain and in the twofold nervous system.

If, as the old Elizabethan poet says, "the soul is form, and doth the body make," then it is clear that the physical organism must be a mechanical arrangement as specially adapted for the use of the soul's powers as a steam engine is for the power of steam. It is the recognition of this reciprocity between the two that is the basis of all spiritual or mental healing. Therefore, the study of this mechanical adaptation is an important branch of Mental Science. Only we must not forget that it is the effect and not the cause.

At the same time, it is important to remember that such a thing as reversal of the relation between cause and effect is possible, just as the same apparatus may be made to generate mechanical power by the application of electricity, or to generate electricity by the application of mechanical power. The importance of this principle consists in this. A tendency always exists for actions that were at first voluntary to become automatic, that is, to pass from the region of conscious mind into that of subconscious mind and to take up residence there. Professor Elmer Gates of Washington has demonstrated this physiologically in his studies of brain formation. He tells us that every thought produces a slight molecular change in the substance of the brain, and the repetition of the same sort of thought causes a repetition of the same molecular action until at last a veritable channel is formed in the brain substance. This can only be eradicated by a reverse process of thought. In this way "grooves of thought" are very literal things. Once established, the vibrations of the cosmic currents flow automatically through them. These currents react upon the mind by the reverse process of that by which our voluntary and intentional in-drawing from the invisible is affected. In this way are formed what we call "habits." Hence the importance of controlling our thinking and guarding it against undesirable ideas.

On the other hand, this reactionary process may be used to confirm good and life-giving modes of thought, so that by a knowledge of its laws we may enlist even the physical body itself in the building up of that perfectly whole personality, the attainment of which is the aim and object of our studies.

XV. THE SOUL

HAVING now obtained a glimpse of the adaptation of the physical organism to the action of the mind, we must next realize that the mind itself is an organism that is in the same way adapted to the action of a still higher power. Only here the adaptation is one of mental faculty. As with other invisible forces, all we can know of the mind is by observing what it does, but with this difference. Since we ourselves are this mind, our observation is an interior observation of states of consciousness. In this way we recognize certain faculties of our mind, the working order of which I have considered earlier. The point to which I would now draw attention is that these faculties always work under the influence of something that stimulates them, and this stimulus may come either from without through the external senses or from within by the consciousness of something not perceptible on the physical plane.

The recognition of these interior sources of stimulus to our mental faculties is an important branch of Mental Science. The mental action thus set up works just as accurately through the corresponding physical impulses as those which start from the recognition of external facts. Therefore, the control and right direction of these inner perceptions is a matter of importance.

The faculties most immediately concerned are the intuition and the imagination, but it is at first difficult to see how intuition, which is entirely spontaneous, can be brought under the control of the will. Of course, the spontaneousness of intuition cannot in any way be interfered with. If it ceased to act spontaneously it would cease to be the intuition. Its province is, as it were, to capture ideas from the infinite and present them to the mind to be dealt with at its discretion. In our mental constitution, the intuition is the point of origination and, therefore, for it to cease to act spontaneously would be for it to cease to act at all. But the experience of a long succession of observers shows that ones intuition can be trained to acquire increased sensitiveness in a particular direction. The choice of direction is determined by the will of the individual.

It will be found that the intuition works most readily in respect to those subjects that most habitually occupy our thought. According to the physiological correspondences that we have been considering, this might be accounted for on the physical plane by the formation of brain channels specially adapted for the induction in the molecular system of vibrations corresponding to the particular class of ideas in question. But of course, we must remember that the ideas themselves are not caused by the molecular changes. On the contrary, they are the cause of them. It is in this translation of thought action into physical action that we are brought face to face with the eternal mystery of the descent of spirit into matter.

We may trace matter through successive degrees of refinement till it becomes what, in comparison with those denser modes that are most familiar, we might call a spiritual substance. Yet at the end of it, it is not the intelligent thinking principle itself. The criterion is in the word "vibrations." However delicately etheric the substance, its movement commences by the vibration of its particles, and a vibration is a wave having a certain length, amplitude, and periodicity. That is to say, something that can exist only in terms of space and time. As soon as we are dealing with anything that can be measured, we may be quite certain that we are not dealing with Spirit, but rather, with one of its vehicles. Therefore, although we may push our analysis of matter further and ever further back — and on this line there is a great deal of knowledge to be gained — we shall find that the point at which spiritual power or thought-force is translated into etheric or atomic vibration will always elude us. Therefore, we must not attribute the origination of ideas to molecular displacement in the brain, though, by the reaction of the physical upon the mental that I have spoken of above, the formation of thought-channels in the gray matter of the brain may tend to facilitate the reception of certain ideas. Some people are actually conscious of the action of the upper portion of the brain during the influx of an intuition, the sensation being that of a sort of expansion in that brain area. This might be compared to the opening of a valve or door. But all attempts to induce the inflow of intuitive ideas by the physiological expedient of trying to open this valve by the exercise of the will should be discouraged as likely to prove injurious to the brain. I believe some Oriental systems advocate this method, but we may well trust the mind to regulate the action of its physical channels in a manner suitable to its own requirements, instead of trying to manipulate the mind by the unnatural forcing of its mechanical instrument. In all our studies on these lines we must remember that development is always by perfectly natural growth and is not brought about by unduly straining any portion of the system.

The fact remains, however, that intuition works most freely in that direction in which we most habitually concentrate our thought. In practice it will be found that the best way to cultivate intuition in any particular direction is to meditate upon the abstract principles of that particular class of subjects rather than only to consider particular cases. Perhaps the reason is that particular cases have to do with specific phenomena, that is with the law working under certain limiting conditions, whereas the principles of the law are not limited by local conditions. So habitual meditation on them sets our intuition free to range in an infinitude where the conception of prior conditions does not limit it. Anyway, whatever may be the theoretical explanation, you will find that the clear grasp of abstract principles in any direction has a wonderfully quickening effect upon the intuition in that particular direction.

The importance of recognizing our power of thus giving direction to the intuition cannot be exaggerated. If the mind is attuned with the highest phases of spirit, this power opens the door to limitless possibilities of knowledge. In its highest workings, intuition becomes inspiration. Certain writings by deep thinkers of old that contain fundamental truths and supreme mysteries can only be accounted for only by supposing that these thinkers earnestly contemplated the Originating Spirit. This was coupled with a reverent worship of the Spirit with the result that the door of their intuitive faculty swung open. Some of the most sublime inspirations regarding the supreme truths of the universe came about — both with respect to the evolution of the cosmos and to the evolution of the individual.

Among such records explaining the supreme mysteries,

three stand out preeminent. All bear witness to the same ONE Truth, and each throw light upon the other. These three are the Bible, the Great Pyramid, and the Pack of Cards — a curious combination some will think, but I hope in another volume of this series to be able to justify my present statement. I allude to these three records here because the unity of principle that they exhibit, notwithstanding their wide divergence of method, affords a standing proof that the direction taken by intuition is largely determined by the will of the individual opening the mind in that particular direction.

Very closely allied to intuition is the faculty of imagination. This does not mean mere fancies, which we dismiss without further consideration, but our power of forming mental images upon which we dwell. These, as I have said in the earlier part of this book, form a nucleus which, on its own plane, calls into action the universal Law of Attraction, thus giving rise to the principle of Growth. The relation of intuition to the imagination is that intuition grasps an idea from the Great Universal Mind, in which all things subsist as potentials. Intuition presents it to the imagination in its essence rather than in a definite form. Then our image building faculty gives it a clear and definite form that it presents before the mental vision, and that we then give life by letting our thought dwell upon it. Thus we infuse our own personality into it, so providing that personal element through which the specific action of the universal law relative to the particular individual always takes place. Whether our thought shall be allowed thus to dwell upon a particular mental image depends on our own will, and our exercise of our will depends on our belief in our power to use it so as to disperse or consolidate a given mental image. Finally, our belief in our power to do this depends on our recognition of our relation to God, Who is the source of all power. For it is an invariable truth that our life will take its whole form, tone, and color from our conception of God, whether that conception be positive or negative, and the sequence by which it does so is that now given.

In this way, then, our intuition is related to our imagination. This relation has its physiological correspondence in the circulus of molecular vibrations I have described above, which, having its commencement in the higher or "ideal" portion of the brain, flows through the voluntary nervous system, which is the physical channel of objective mind. It returns through the sympathetic system, the physical channel of subjective mind, thus completing the circuit. Being then restored to the frontal brain, it is consciously modeled into clear-cut forms suited to a specific purpose.

In all this, the power of the will in regulating the action both of intuition and imagination must never be lost sight of. Without such a central controlling power, we should lose all sense of individuality. Hence the ultimate aim of the evolutionary process is to evolve individual wills actuated by such beneficence and enlightenment as shall make them fitting vehicles for the out-flowing of the Supreme Spirit, which has hitherto created cosmically, and can now carry on the creative process to its highest stages only through conscious union with the individual. This is the only possible solution to the great problem, "How can the Universal Mind act in all its fullness upon the plane of the individual and particular?"

This is the ultimate goal of evolution, and the successful evolution of the individual depends on his recognizing this ultimate goal and working towards it. Therefore, this should be the major objective of our studies. A correspondence exists in the constitution of the body to the faculties of the soul, and a similar correspondence exists in the faculties of the soul to the power of the All-originating Spirit. As in all other adaptations of specific vehicles, we can never correctly understand the nature of the vehicle and use it rightly until we realize the nature of the power for the working of which it is specially adapted. Let us, then, in conclusion briefly consider the nature of that power.

XVI. THE SPIRIT

WHAT must the Supreme All-originating Spirit be in itself? That is the question before us. Let us start with one fact regarding it about which we cannot have doubt — it is creative. If it were not creative, nothing could come into existence. Therefore, we know that its purpose, or Law of Tendency, must be to bring individual lives into existence and to surround them with a suitable environment. A power that has this inherent nature must be a kindly power. The Spirit of Life seeking expression in individual lives can have no other intention towards them than "that they might have life, and that they might have it more abundantly." To suppose the opposite would be a contradiction in terms. It would be to suppose the Eternal Principle of Life acting against itself, expressing itself as the reverse of what it is, in which case it would not be expressing itself but expressing its opposite.

It is impossible to conceive of the Spirit of Life acting otherwise than to the increase of life. This is as yet only imperfectly apparent because of our imperfect understanding of the position, and our consequential lack of conscious unity with the ONE Eternal Life. As our consciousness of unity becomes more perfect, so will the life-giving-ness of the Spirit become more apparent. But in the realm of principles, the purely Affirmative and Life-giving nature of the All-originating Spirit is an unavoidable conclusion.

Now by what name can we call such an inherent desire to add to the fullness of any individual life — that is, to make it stronger, brighter, and happier? If this is not Love, then I do not know what else it is. So we are philosophically led to the conclusion that Love is the prime moving power of the Creating Spirit. Expression is, however, impossible without Form. What Form, then, should Love give to the vehicles of its expression? By the hypothesis of the case it could not find self-expression in forms that were hateful or repugnant to it — therefore the only logical correlative of Love is Beauty. Beauty is not yet universally manifested for the same reason that Life is not, namely, lack of recognition of its Principle. But that the principle of Beauty is inherent in the Eternal Mind is demonstrated by all that is beautiful in the world in which we live.

These considerations show us that the inherent nature of the Spirit must consist in the eternal interaction of Love and Beauty as the Active and Passive polarity of Being. This, then, is the Power for the working of which our soul faculties are specially adapted. When this purpose of the adaptation is recognized, we begin to get some insight into the way in which our intuition, imagination and will should be exercised. By training our thought to habitually dwell upon the dual unity of the Originating Forces of Love and Beauty, the intuition is rendered more and more sensitive to ideas emanating from this supreme source. At the same time, the imagining faculty is trained in the formation of images corresponding to such ideas, and on the physical side, the molecular structure of the brain and body becomes more and more perfectly adjusted to the generating of vibratory currents tending to the outward manifestation of the Originating Principle. Thus the whole man is brought into unison with himself and with the Supreme Source of Life, so that, in the words of St. Paul, he is being day by day renewed after the image of Him that created him.

Our more immediately personal recognition of the All-originating Love and Beauty will thus flow out as peace of mind, health of body, discretion in the management of our affairs, and power in the carrying out of our undertakings. As we advance to a wider conception of the working of the Spirit of Love and Beauty in its infinite possibilities, so our intuition will find a wider scope and our field of activity will expand along with it. In a word, we shall discover that our individuality is growing and that we are becoming more truly ourselves than we ever were before.

Of supreme importance is the question of the specific lines along which the individual may be most perfectly trained into such recognition of his true relation to the All-embracing Spirit of Life. It is of such magnitude that even to briefly sketch its broad outlines would require a volume to itself. I will therefore not attempt to enter upon it here. My present purpose is only to offer some hints of the principles underlying that wonderful threefold unity of Body, Mind and Spirit which we all know ourselves to be.

We are as yet only at the beginning of the path that leads to the realization of this unity in the full development of all its powers, but others have trodden the way before us. We may learn from them. Not least among these was the illustrious founder of the Most Christian Fraternity of the Rosicrucians. This mastermind, setting out in his youth with the intention of going to Jerusalem, changed the order of his journey and first sojourned for three years in the symbolic city of Damcar, in the mystical country of Arabia. Then he spent about a year in the mystical country of Egypt. Then two years in the mystical country of Fez. Having during these six years learned all that was to be acquired in those countries, he returned to his native land of Germany, where, on the basis of the knowledge he had thus gained, he founded the Fraternity R. C., for whose instruction he wrote the mystical books M. and T.

When he realized that his work in its present stage was accomplished, he of his own free will laid aside the physical body, not, it is recorded, by decay, or disease, or ordinary death, but by the express direction of the Spirit of Life, summing up all his knowledge in the words,

"Jesus mihi omnia."

And now his followers await the coming of "the Artist Elias," who shall bring the Magnum Opus to its completion.

"Let him that readeth understand."

As A Man Thinketh

by James Allen

(Circa 1905)

Foreword

This little volume (the result of meditation and experience) is not intended as an exhaustive treatise on the much-written upon subject of the power of thought. It is suggestive rather than explanatory, its object being to stimulate men and women to the discovery and perception of the truth that -

"They themselves are makers of themselves" by virtue of the thoughts which they choose and encourage; that mind is the master weaver, both of the inner garment of character and the outer garment of circumstance, and that, as they may have hitherto woven in ignorance and pain they may now weave in enlightenment and happiness.

James Allen

Chapter One
Thought and Character

The aphorism, "As a man thinketh in his heart so is he," not only embraces the whole of a man's being, but is so comprehensive as to reach out to every condition and circumstance of his life. A man is literally *what he thinks*, his character being the complete sum of all his thoughts.

As the plant springs from, and could not be without, the seed, so every act of a man springs from the hidden seeds of thought, and could not have appeared without them. This applies equally to those acts called "spontaneous" and "unpremeditated" as to those which are deliberately executed.

Act is the blossom of thought, and joy and suffering are its fruits; thus does a man garner in the sweet and bitter fruitage of his own husbandry.

Thought in the mind hath made us. What we are
By thought we wrought and built. If a man's mind
Hath evil thoughts, pain comes on him as comes
The wheel the ox behind . . . If one endure in purity
of thought joy follows him as his own shadow - sure.

Man is a growth by law, and not a creation by artifice, and cause and effect is as absolute and undeviating in the hidden realm of thought as in the world of visible and material things. A noble and Godlike character is not a thing of favor or chance, but is the natural result of continued effort in right thinking, the effect of long-cherished association with Godlike thoughts. An ignoble and bestial character, by the same process, is the result of the continued harboring of groveling thoughts.

Man is made or unmade by himself; in the armory of thought he forges the weapons by which he destroys himself. He also fashions the tools with which he builds for himself heavenly mansions of joy and strength and peace. By the right choice and true application of thought, man ascends to the Divine Perfection; by the abuse and wrong application of thought, he descends below the level of the beast. Between these two extremes are all the grades of character, and man is their maker and master.

Of all the beautiful truths pertaining to the soul which have been restored and brought to light in this age, none is more gladdening or fruitful of divine promise and confidence than this - that man is the master of thought, the molder of character, and maker and shaper of condition, environment, and destiny.

As a being of Power, Intelligence, and Love, and the lord of his own thoughts, man holds the key to every situation, and contains within himself that transforming and regenerative agency by which he may make himself what he wills.

Man is always the master, even in his weakest and most abandoned state; but in his weakness and degradation he is the foolish master who misgoverns his "household." When he begins to reflect upon his condition, and to search diligently for the Law upon which his being is established, he then becomes the wise master, directing his energies with intelligence, and fashioning his thoughts to fruitful issues. Such is the *conscious* master, and man can only thus become by discovering *within himself* the laws of thought; which discovery is totally a matter of application, self-analysis, and experience.

Only by much searching and mining are gold and diamonds obtained, and man can find every truth connected with his being if he will dig deep into the mine of his soul. And that he is the maker of his character, the molder of his life, and the builder of his destiny, he may unerringly prove: if he will watch, control, and alter his thoughts, tracing their effects upon himself, upon others, and upon his life and circumstances; if he will link cause and effect by patient practice and investigation, utilizing his every experience, even to the most trivial, as a means of obtaining that knowledge of himself. In this direction, as in no other, is the law absolute that "He that seeketh findeth; and to him that knocketh it shall be opened"; for only by patience, practice, and ceaseless importunity can a man enter the Door of the Temple of Knowledge.

Chapter Two
Effect of Thought on Circumstances

A man's mind may be likened to a garden, which may be intelligently cultivated or allowed to run wild; but whether cultivated or neglected, it must, and will, *bring forth*. If no useful seeds are *put* into it, then an abundance of useless weed seeds will *fall* therein, and will continue to produce their kind.

Just as a gardener cultivates his plot, keeping it free from weeds, and growing the flowers and fruits which he requires, so may a man tend the garden of his mind, weeding out all the wrong, useless, and impure thoughts, and cultivating toward perfection the flowers and fruits of right, useful, and pure thoughts. By pursuing this process, a man sooner or later discovers that he is the master gardener of his soul, the director of his life. He also reveals, within himself, the laws of thought, and understands with ever-increasing accuracy how the thought forces and mind elements operate in the shaping of his character, circumstances, and destiny.

Thought and character are one, and as character can only manifest and discover itself through environment and circumstance, the outer conditions of a person's life will always be found to be harmoniously related to his inner state. This does not mean that a man's circumstances at any given time are an indication of his *entire* character, but that those circumstances are so intimately connected with some vital thought element within himself that, for the time being, they are indispensable to his development.

Every man is where he is by the law of his being. The thoughts which he has built into his character have brought him there, and in the arrangement of his life there is no element of chance, but all is the result of a law which cannot err. This is just as true of those who feel "out of harmony" with their surroundings as of those who are contented with them.

As the progressive and evolving being, man is where he is that he may learn that he may grow; and as he learns the spiritual lesson which any circumstance contains for him, it passes away and gives place to other circumstances.

Man is buffeted by circumstances so long as he believes himself to be the creature of outside conditions. But when he realizes that he may command the hidden soil and seeds of his being out of which circumstances grow, he then becomes the rightful master of himself.

That circumstances *grow* out of thought every man knows who has for any length of time practiced self-control and self-purification, for he will have noticed that the alteration in his circumstances has been in exact ratio with his altered mental condition. So true is this that when a man earnestly applies himself to remedy the defects in his character, and makes swift and marked progress, he passes rapidly through a succession of vicissitudes.

The soul attracts that which it secretly harbors; that which it loves, and also that which it fears. It reaches the height of its cherished aspirations. It falls to the level of its unchastened desires - and circumstances are the means by which the soul receives its own.

Every thought seed sown or allowed to fall into the mind, and to take root there, produces its own, blossoming sooner or later into act, and bearing its own fruitage of opportunity and circumstance. Good thoughts bear good fruit, bad thoughts bad fruit.

The outer world of circumstance shapes itself to the inner world of thought, and both pleasant and unpleasant external conditions are factors which make for the ultimate good of the individual. As the reaper of his own harvest, man learns both by suffering and bliss.

A man does not come to the almshouse or the jail by the tyranny of fate of circumstance, but by the pathway of groveling thoughts and base desires. Nor does a pure-minded man fall suddenly into crime by stress of any mere external force; the criminal thought had long been secretly fostered in the heart, and the hour of opportunity revealed its gathered power.

Circumstance does not make the man; it reveals him to himself. No such conditions can exist as descending into vice and its attendant sufferings apart from vicious inclinations, or ascending into virtue and its pure happiness without the continued cultivation of virtuous aspirations. And man, therefore, as the Lord and master of thought, is the maker of himself, the shaper and author of environment. Even at birth the soul comes to its own, and through every step of its earthly pilgrimage it attracts those combinations of conditions which reveal itself, which are the reflections of its own purity and impurity, its strength and weakness.

Men do not attract that which they *want*, but that which they *are*. Their whims, fancies, and ambitions are thwarted at every step, but their inmost thoughts and desires are fed with their own food, be it foul or clean. The "divinity that shapes our ends" is in ourselves; it is our very self. Man is manacled only by himself. Thought and action are the jailers of Fate -

they imprison, being base. They are also the angels of Freedom - they liberate, being noble. Not what he wishes and prays for does a man get, but what he justly earns. His wishes and prayers are only gratified and answered when they harmonize with his thoughts and actions.

In the light of this truth, what, then, is the meaning of "fighting against circumstances"? It means that a man is continually revolting against an *effect* without, while all the time he is nourishing and preserving its *cause* in his heart. That cause may take the form of a conscious vice or an unconscious weakness; but whatever it is, it stubbornly retards the efforts of its possessor, and thus calls aloud for remedy.

Men are anxious to improve their circumstances, but are unwilling to improve themselves. They therefore remain bound. The man who does not shrink from self-crucifixion can never fail to accomplish the object upon which his heart is set. This is as true of earthly as of heavenly things. Even the man whose sole object is to acquire wealth must be prepared to make great personal sacrifices before he can accomplish his object; and how much more so he who would realize a strong and well-poised life?

Here is a man who is wretchedly poor. He is extremely anxious that his surroundings and home comforts should be improved. Yet all the time he shirks his work, and considers he is justified in trying to deceive his employer on the ground of the insufficiency of his wages. Such a man does not understand the simplest rudiments of those principles which are the basis of true prosperity. He is not only totally unfitted to rise out of his wretchedness, but is actually attracting to himself a still deeper wretchedness by dwelling in, and acting out, indolent, deceptive, and unmanly thoughts.

Here is a rich man who is the victim of a painful and persistent disease as the result of gluttony. He is willing to give large sums of money to get rid of it, but he will not sacrifice his gluttonous desires. He wants to gratify his taste for rich and unnatural foods and have his health as well. Such a man is totally unfit to have health, because he has not yet learned the first principles of a healthy life.

Here is an employer of labor who adopts crooked measures to avoid paying the regulation wage, and, in the hope of making larger profits, reduces the wages of his workpeople. Such a man is altogether unfitted for prosperity. And when he finds himself bankrupt, both as regards reputation and riches, he blames circumstances, not knowing that he is the sole author of his condition.

I have introduced these three cases merely as illustrative of the truth that man is the cause (though nearly always unconsciously) of his circumstances. That, while aiming at the good end, he is continually frustrating its accomplishment by encouraging thoughts and desires which cannot possibly harmonize with that end. Such cases could be multiplied and varied almost indefinitely, but this is not necessary. The reader can, if he so resolves, trace the action of the laws of thought in his own mind and life, and until this is done, mere external facts cannot serve as a ground of reasoning.

Circumstances, however, are so complicated, thought is so deeply rooted, and the conditions of happiness vary so vastly with individuals, that a man's *entire* soul condition (although it may be known to himself) cannot be judged by another from the external aspect of his life alone.

A man may be honest in certain directions, yet suffer privations. A man may be dishonest in certain directions, yet acquire wealth. But the conclusion usually formed that the one man fails *because of his particular honesty,* and that the other prospers *because of his particular dishonesty,* is the result of a superficial judgment, which assumes that the dishonest man is almost totally corrupt, and the honest man almost entirely virtuous. In the light of a deeper knowledge and wider experience, such judgment is found to be erroneous. The dishonest man may have some admirable virtues which the other does not possess; and the honest man obnoxious vices which are absent in the other. The honest man reaps the good results of his honest thoughts and acts; he also brings upon himself the sufferings which his vices produce. The dishonest man likewise garners his own suffering and happiness.

It is pleasing to human vanity to believe that one suffers because of one's virtue. But not until a man has extirpated every sickly, bitter, and impure thought from his mind, and washed every sinful stain from his soul, can he be in a position to know and declare that his sufferings are the result of his good, and not of his bad qualities. And on the way to that supreme perfection, he will have found working in his mind and life, the Great Law which is absolutely just, and which cannot give good for evil, evil for good. Possessed of such knowledge, he will then know, looking back upon his past ignorance and blindness, that his life is, and always was, justly ordered, and that all his past experiences, good and bad, were the equitable outworking of his evolving, yet unevolved self.

Good thoughts and actions can never produce bad results. Bad thoughts and actions can never produce good results. This is but saying that nothing can come from corn but corn, nothing from nettles but nettles. Men understand this law in the natural world, and work with it. But few understand it in the mental and moral world (though its operation there is just as simple and undeviating), and they, therefore, do not cooperate with it.

Suffering is *always* the effect of wrong thought in some direction. It is an indication that the individual is out of harmony with himself, with the Law of his being. The sole and supreme use of suffering is to purify, to burn out all that is useless and impure. Suffering ceases for him who is pure. There could be no object in burning gold after the dross had been removed, and perfectly pure and enlightened being could not suffer.

The circumstances which a man encounters with suffering are the result of his own mental inharmony. The circumstances which a man encounters with blessedness, not material possessions, is the measure of right thought. Wretchedness, not lack of material possessions, is the measure of wrong thought. A man may be cursed and rich; he may be blessed and poor. Blessedness and riches are only joined together when the riches are rightly and wisely used. And the poor man only descends into wretchedness when he regards his lot as a burden unjustly imposed.

Indigence and indulgence are the two extremes of wretchedness. They are both equally unnatural and the result of mental disorder. A man is not rightly conditioned until he is a happy, healthy, and prosperous being. And happiness, health, and prosperity are the result of a harmonious adjustment of the inner with the outer, of the man with his surroundings.

A man only begins to be a man when he ceases to whine and revile, and commences to search for the hidden justice which regulates his life. And as he adapts his mind to that regulating factor, he ceases to accuse others as the cause of his condition, and builds himself up in strong and noble thoughts. He ceases to kick against circumstances, but begins to *use* them as aids to his more rapid progress, and as a means of discovering the hidden powers and possibilities within himself.

Law, not confusion, is the dominating principle in the universe. Justice, not injustice, is the soul and substance of life. And righteousness, not corruption, is the molding and moving force in the spiritual government of the world. This being so, man has but to right himself to find that the universe is right; and during the process of putting himself right, he will find that as he alters his thoughts toward things and other people, things and other people will alter toward him.

The proof of this truth is in every person, and it therefore admits of easy investigation by systematic introspection and self-analysis. Let a man radically alter his thoughts, and he will be astonished at the rapid transformation it will effect in the material conditions of his life.

Men imagine that thought can be kept secret, but it cannot. It rapidly crystallizes into habit, and habit solidifies into habits of drunkenness and sensuality, which solidify into circumstances of destitution and disease. Impure thoughts of every kind crystallize into enervating and confusing habits, which solidify into distracting and adverse circumstances. Thoughts of fear, doubt, and indecision crystallize into weak, unmanly, and irresolute habits, which solidify into circumstances of failure, indigence, and slavish dependence.

Lazy thoughts crystallize into habits of uncleanliness and dishonesty, which solidify into circumstances of foulness and beggary. Hateful and condemnatory thoughts crystallize into habits of accusation and violence, which solidify into circumstances of injury and persecution. Selfish thoughts of all kinds crystallize into habits of self-seeking, which solidify into circumstances more or less distressing.

On the other hand, beautiful thoughts of all crystallize into habits of grace and kindliness, which solidify into genial and sunny circumstances. Pure thoughts crystallize into habits of temperance and self-control, which solidify into circumstances of repose and peace. Thoughts of courage, self-reliance, and decision crystallize into manly habits, which solidify into circumstances of success, plenty, and freedom.

Energetic thoughts crystallize into habits of cleanliness and industry, which solidify into circumstances of pleasantness. Gentle and forgiving thoughts crystallize into habits of gentleness, which solidify into protective and preservative circumstances. Loving and unselfish thoughts crystallize into habits of self-forgetfulness for others, which solidify into circumstances of sure and abiding prosperity and true riches.

A particular train of thought persisted in, be it good or bad, cannot fail to produce its results on the character and circumstances. A man cannot *directly* choose his circumstances, but he can choose his thoughts, and so indirectly, yet surely, shape his circumstances.

Nature helps every man to the gratification of the thoughts which he most encourages, and opportunities are presented which will most speedily bring to the surface both the good and evil thoughts.

Let a man cease from his sinful thoughts, and all the world will soften toward him, and be ready to help him. Let him put away his weakly and sickly thoughts, and lo! opportunities will spring up on every hand to aid his strong resolves. Let him encourage good thoughts, and no hard fate shall bind him down to wretchedness and shame. The world is your kaleidoscope, and the varying combinations of colors which at every succeeding moment it presents to you are the exquisitely adjusted pictures of your ever moving thoughts.

You will be what you will to be;
Let failure find its false content
In that poor word, "environment,"
But spirit scorns it, and is free.
It masters time, it conquers space;
It cows that boastful trickster, Chance,
And bids the tyrant Circumstance
Uncrown, and fill a servant's place.
The human Will, that force unseen,
The offspring of a deathless Soul,
Can hew a way to any goal,
Though walls of granite intervene.
Be not impatient in delay,
But wait as one who understands;
When spirit rises and commands,
The gods are ready to obey.

Chapter Three
Effect of Thought on Health and the Body

The body is the servant of the mind. It obeys the operations of the mind, whether they be deliberately chosen or automatically expressed. At the bidding of unlawful thoughts the body sinks rapidly into disease and decay; at the command of glad and beautiful thoughts it becomes clothed with youthfulness and beauty.

Disease and health, like circumstances, are rooted in thought. Sickly thoughts will express themselves through a sickly body. Thoughts of fear have been known to kill a man as speedily as a bullet, and they are continually killing thousands of people just as surely though less rapidly. The people who live in fear of disease are the people who get it. Anxiety quickly demoralizes the whole body, and lays it open to the entrance of disease; while impure thoughts, even if not physically indulged, will soon shatter the nervous system.

Strong, pure, and happy thoughts build up the body in vigor and grace. The body is a delicate and plastic instrument, which responds readily to the thoughts by which it is impressed, and habits of thought will produce their own effects, good or bad, upon it.

Men will continue to have impure and poisoned blood so long as they propagate unclean thoughts. Out of a clean heart comes a clean life and a clean body. Out of a defiled mind proceeds a defiled life and corrupt body. Thought is the fountain of action, life and manifestation; make the fountain pure, and all will be pure.

Change of diet will not help a man who will not change his thoughts. When a man makes his thoughts pure, he no longer desires impure food.

If you would perfect your body, guard your mind. If you would renew your body, beautify your mind. Thoughts of malice, envy, disappointment, despondency, rob the body of its health and grace. A sour face does not come by chance; it is made by sour thoughts. Wrinkles that mar are drawn by folly, passion, pride.

I know a woman of ninety-six who has the bright, innocent face of a girl. I know a man well under middle age whose face is drawn into inharmonious contours. The one is the result of a sweet and sunny disposition; the other is the outcome of passion and discontent.

As you cannot have a sweet and wholesome abode unless you admit the air and sunshine freely into your rooms, so a strong body and a bright, happy, or serene countenance can only result from the free admittance into the mind of thoughts of joy and good will and serenity.

On the faces of the aged there are wrinkles made by sympathy, others by strong and pure thought, others are carved by passion. Who cannot distinguish them? With those who have lived righteously, age is calm, peaceful, and softly mellowed, like the setting sun. I have recently seen a philosopher on his deathbed. He was not old except in years. He died as sweetly and peacefully as he had lived.

There is no physician like cheerful thought for dissipating the ills of the body; there is no comforter to compare with good will for dispersing the shadows of grief and sorrow. To live continually in thoughts of ill will, cynicism, suspicion, and envy, is to be confined in a self-made prison hole. But to think well of all, to be cheerful with all, to patiently learn to find the good in all - such unselfish thoughts are the very portals of heaven; and to dwell day to day in thoughts of peace toward every creature will bring abounding peace to their possessor.

Chapter Four
Thought and Purpose

Until thought is linked with purpose there is no intelligent accomplishment. With the majority the bark of thought is allowed to "drift" upon the ocean of life. Aimlessness is a vice, and such drifting must not continue for him who would steer clear of catastrophe and destruction.

They who have no central purpose in their life fall an easy prey to worries, fears, troubles, and self-pityings, all of which are indications of weakness, which lead, just as surely as deliberately planned sins (though by a different route), to failure, unhappiness, and loss, for weakness cannot persist in a power-evolving universe.

A man should conceive of a legitimate purpose in his heart, and set out to accomplish it. He should make this purpose the centralizing point of his thoughts. It may take the form of a spiritual ideal, or it may be a worldly object, according to his nature at the time being. But whichever it is, he should steadily focus his thought forces upon the object which he has set before him. He should make this purpose his supreme duty, and should devote himself to its attainment, not allowing his thoughts to wander away into ephemeral fancies, longings, and imaginings. This is the royal road to self-control and true concentration of thought. Even if he fails again and again to accomplish his purpose (as he necessarily must until weakness is overcome), the *strength of character gained* will be the measure of his *true* success, and this will form a new starting point for future power and triumph.

Those who are not prepared for the apprehension of a *great* purpose, should fix the thoughts upon the faultless performance of their duty, no matter how insignificant their task may appear. Only in this way can the thoughts be gathered and focused, and resolution and energy be developed, which being done, there is nothing which may not be accomplished.

The weakest soul, knowing its own weakness, and believing this truth - *that strength can only be developed by effort and practice,* will at once begin to exert itself, and adding effort to effort, patience to patience, and strength to strength, will never cease to develop, and will at last grow divinely strong.

As the physically weak man can make himself strong by careful and patient training, so the man of weak thoughts can make them strong by exercising himself in right thinking.

To put away aimlessness and weakness, and to begin to think with purpose, is to enter the ranks of those strong ones who only recognize failure as one of the pathways to attainment; who make all conditions serve them, and who think strongly, attempt fearlessly, and accomplish masterfully.

Having conceived of his purpose, a man should mentally mark out a *straight* pathway to its achievement, looking neither to the right nor to the left. Doubts and fears should be rigorously excluded; they are disintegrating elements which break up the straight line of effort, rendering it crooked, ineffectual, useless. Thoughts of doubt and fear never accomplish anything, and never can. They always lead to failure. Purpose, energy, power to do, and all strong thoughts cease when doubt and fear creep in.

The will to do springs from the knowledge that we *can* do.

Doubt and fear are the great enemies of knowledge, and he who encourages them, who does not slay them, thwarts himself at every step.

He who has conquered doubt and fear has conquered failure. His every thought is allied with power, and all difficulties are bravely met and wisely overcome. His purposes are seasonably planted, and they bloom and bring forth fruit which does not fall prematurely to the ground.

Thought allied fearlessly to purpose becomes creative force. He who *knows* this is ready to become something higher and stronger than a mere bundle of wavering thoughts and fluctuating sensations. He who *does* this has become the conscious and intelligent wielder of his mental powers.

Chapter Five
The Thought-Factor in Achievement

All that a man achieves and all that he fails to achieve is
the direct result of his own thoughts. In a justly ordered
universe, where loss of equipoise would mean total
destruction, individual responsibility must be absolute. A
man's weakness and strength, purity and impurity, are his
own, and not another man's. They are brought about by
himself, and not by another; and they can only be altered by
himself, never by another. His condition is also his own, and
not another man's. His suffering and his happiness are
evolved from within. As he thinks, so he is; as he continues to
think, so he remains.

A strong man cannot help a weaker unless the weaker is
willing to be helped, and even then the weak man must become
strong of himself. He must, by his own efforts, develop the
strength which he admires in another. None but himself can
alter his condition.

It has been usual for men to think and to say, "Many men
are slaves because one is an oppressor; let us hate the
oppressor." Now, however, there is among an increasing few a
tendency to reverse this judgment, and to say, "One man is an
oppressor because many are slaves; let us despise the slaves."
The truth is that oppressor and slave are cooperators in
ignorance, and, while seeming to afflict each other, are in
reality afflicting themselves. A perfect Knowledge perceives
the action of law in the weakness of the oppressed and the

misapplied power of the oppressor. A perfect Love, seeing the suffering which both states entail, condemns neither. A perfect Compassion embraces both oppressor and oppressed.

He who has conquered weakness, and has put away all selfish thoughts, belongs neither to oppressor nor oppressed. He is free.

A man can only rise, conquer, and achieve by lifting up his thoughts. He can only remain weak, and abject, and miserable by refusing to lift up his thoughts.

Before a man can achieve anything, even in worldly things, he must lift his thoughts above slavish animal indulgence. He may not, in order to succeed, give up *all* animality and selfishness, by any means; but a portion of it must, at least, be sacrificed. A man whose first thought is bestial indulgence could neither think clearly nor plan methodically. He could not find and develop his latent resources, and would fail in any undertaking. Not having commenced manfully to control his thoughts, he is not in a position to control affairs and to adopt serious responsibilities. He is not fit to act independently and stand alone, but he is limited only by the thoughts which he chooses.

There can be no progress, no achievement without sacrifice. A man's worldly success will be in the measure that he sacrifices his confused animal thoughts, and fixes his mind on the development of his plans, and the strengthening of his resolution and self reliance. And the higher he lifts his thoughts, the more manly, upright, and righteous he becomes, the greater will be his success, the more blessed and enduring will be his achievements.

The universe does not favor the greedy, the dishonest, the vicious, although on the mere surface it may sometimes appear to do so; it helps the honest, the magnanimous, the virtuous. All the great Teachers of the ages have declared this in varying forms, and to prove and know it a man has but to persist in making himself more and more virtuous by lifting up his thoughts.

Intellectual achievements are the result of thought consecrated to the search for knowledge, or for the beautiful and true in life and nature. Such achievements may be sometimes connected with vanity and ambition but they are not the outcome of those characteristics. They are the natural outgrowth of long and arduous effort, and of pure and unselfish thoughts.

Spiritual achievements are the consummation of holy aspirations. He who lives constantly in the conception of noble and lofty thoughts, who dwells upon all that is pure and unselfish, will, as surely as the sun reaches its zenith and the moon its full, become wise and noble in character, and rise into a position of influence and blessedness.

Achievement, of whatever kind, is the crown of effort, the diadem of thought. By the aid of self-control, resolution, purity, righteousness, and well-directed thought a man ascends. By the aid of animality, indolence, impurity, corruption, and confusion of thought a man descends.

A man may rise to high success in the world, and even to lofty altitudes in the spiritual realm, and again descend into weakness and wretchedness by allowing arrogant, selfish, and corrupt thoughts to take possession of him.

Victories attained by right thought can only be maintained by watchfulness. Many give way when success is assured, and rapidly fall back into failure.

All achievements, whether in the business, intellectual, or

spiritual world, are the result of definitely directed thought, are governed by the same law and are of the same method; the only difference lies in *the object of attainment.*

He who would accomplish little must sacrifice little. He who would achieve much must sacrifice much. He who would attain highly must sacrifice greatly.

Chapter Six
Visions and Ideals

The dreamers are the saviors of the world. As the visible world is sustained by the invisible, so men, through all their trials and sins and sordid vocations, are nourished by the beautiful visions of their solitary dreamers. Humanity cannot forget its dreamers. It cannot let their ideals fade and die. It lives in them. It knows them in the *realities* which it shall one day see and know.

Composer, sculptor, painter, poet, prophet, sage, these are the makers of the afterworld, the architects of heaven. The world is beautiful because they have lived; without them, laboring humanity would perish.

He who cherishes a beautiful vision, a lofty ideal in his heart, will one day realize it. Columbus cherished a vision of another world, and he discovered it. Copernicus fostered the vision of a multiplicity of worlds and a wider universe, and he revealed it. Buddha beheld the vision of a spiritual world of stainless beauty and perfect peace, and he entered into it.

Cherish your visions. Cherish your ideals. Cherish the music that stirs in your heart, the beauty that forms in your mind, the loveliness that drapes your purest thoughts, for out of them will grow all delightful conditions, all heavenly environment; of these, if you but remain true to them, your world will at last be built.

To desire is to obtain; to aspire is to achieve. Shall man's basest desires receive the fullest measure of gratification, and his purest aspirations starve for lack of sustenance? Such is not the Law. Such a condition of things can never obtain - "Ask and receive."

Dream lofty dreams, and as you dream, so shall you become. Your Vision is the promise of what you shall one day be. Your Ideal is the prophecy of what you shall at last unveil.

The greatest achievement was at first and for a time a dream. The oak sleeps in the acorn; the bird waits in the egg; and in the highest vision of the soul a waking angel stirs. Dreams are the seedlings of realities.

Your circumstances may be uncongenial, but they shall not long remain so if you but perceive an Ideal and strive to reach it. You cannot travel *within* and stand still *without*. Here is a youth hard pressed by poverty and labor; confined long hours in an unhealthy workshop; unschooled, and lacking all the arts of refinement. But he dreams of better things. He thinks of intelligence, of refinement, of grace and beauty. He conceives of, mentally builds up, an ideal condition of life. The vision of the wider liberty and a larger scope takes possession of him; unrest urges him to action, and he utilizes all his spare time and means, small though they are, to the development of his latent powers and resources.

Very soon, so altered has his mind become that the workshop can no longer hold him. It has become so out of harmony with his mentality that it falls out of his life as a garment is cast aside, and with the growth of opportunities which fit the scope of his expanding powers, he passes out of it forever.

Years later we see this youth as a full-grown man. We find him a master of certain forces of the mind which he wields with worldwide influence and almost unequaled power. In his hands he holds the cords of gigantic responsibilities. He speaks, and lo! lives are changed. Men and women hang upon his words and remold their characters, and, sunlike, he becomes the fixed and luminous center around which innumerable destinies revolve. He has realized the Vision of his youth. He has become one with his Ideal.

And you, too, youthful reader, will realize the Vision (not the idle wish) of your heart, be it base or beautiful, or a mixture of both, for you will always gravitate toward that which you secretly most love. Into your hands will be placed the exact results of your own thoughts; you will receive that which you earn, no more, no less. Whatever your present environment may be, you will fall, remain, or rise with your thoughts, your Vision, your Ideal. You will become as small as your controlling desire; as great as your dominant aspiration.

In the beautiful words of Stanton Kirkham Dave:

> You may be keeping accounts, and presently
> you shall walk out of the door that for so long
> has seemed to you the barrier of your ideals,
> and shall find yourself before an audience - the
> pen still behind your ear, the ink stains on your
> fingers - and then and there shall pour out the
> torrent of your inspiration. You may be driving
> sheep, and you shall wander to the city -
> bucolic and open mouthed; shall wander under
> the intrepid guidance of the spirit into the
> studio of the master, and after a time he shall
> say, 'I have nothing more to teach you.' And
> now you have become the master, who did so
> recently dream of great things while driving
> sheep. You shall lay down the saw and the
> plane to take upon yourself the regeneration of
> the world.

The thoughtless, the ignorant, and the indolent, seeing only the apparent effects of things and not the things themselves, talk of luck, of fortune, and chance. See a man grow rich, they say, "How lucky he is!" Observing another become intellectual, they exclaim, "How highly favored he is!" And noting the saintly character and wide influence of another, the remark, "How chance aids him at every turn!"

They do not see the trials and failures and struggles which these men have voluntarily encountered in order to gain their experience. They have no knowledge of the sacrifices they have made, of the undaunted efforts they have put forth, of the faith they have exercised, that they might overcome the apparently insurmountable, and realize the Vision of their heart. They do not know the darkness and the heartaches; they only see the light and joy, and call it "luck"; do not see the long and arduous journey, but only behold the pleasant goal, and call it "good fortune"; do not understand the process, but only perceive the result, and call it "chance."

In all human affairs there are *efforts*, and there are *results*, and the strength of the effort is the measure of the result. Chance is not. "Gifts," powers, material, intellectual, and spiritual possessions are the fruits of effort. They are thoughts completed, objects accomplished, visions realized.

The vision that you glorify in your mind, the Ideal that you enthrone in your heart - this you will build your life by, this you will become.

Chapter Seven
Serenity

Calmness of mind is one of the beautiful jewels of wisdom.
It is the result of long and patient effort in self-control. Its
presence is an indication of ripened experience, and of a more
than ordinary knowledge of the laws and operations of
thought.

A man becomes calm in the measure that he understands
himself as a thought-evolved being, for such knowledge
necessitates the understanding of others as the result of
thought. As he develops a right understanding, and sees more
and more clearly the internal relations of things by the action
of cause and effect, he ceases to fuss and fume and worry and
grieve, and remains poised, steadfast, serene.

The calm man, having learned how to govern himself,
knows how to adapt himself to others; and they, in turn,
reverence his spiritual strength, and feel that they can learn of
him and rely upon him. The more tranquil a man becomes, the
greater is his success, his influence, his power for good. Even
the ordinary trader will find his business prosperity increase
as he develops a greater self-control and equanimity, for
people will always prefer to deal with a man whose demeanor
is strongly equable.

The strong calm man is always loved and revered. He is
like a shade-giving tree in a thirsty land, or a sheltering rock in
a storm. Who does not love a tranquil heart, a sweet-
tempered, balanced life? It does not matter whether it rains or
shines, or what changes come to those possessing these
blessings, for they are always sweet, serene, and calm. That

exquisite poise of character which we call serenity is the last lesson culture; it is the flowering of life, the fruitage of the soul. It is precious as wisdom, more to be desired than gold - yea, than even fine gold. How insignificant mere money-seeking looks in comparison with a serene life - a life that dwells in the ocean of Truth, beneath the waves, beyond the reach of tempests, in the Eternal Calm!

> How many people we know who sour their lives, who ruin all that is sweet and beautiful by explosive tempers, who destroy their poise of character, and make bad blood! It is a question whether the great majority of people do not ruin their lives and mar their happiness by lack of self-control. How few people we meet in life who are well-balanced, who have that exquisite poise which is characteristic of the finished character!

Yes, humanity surges with uncontrolled passion, is tumultuous with ungoverned grief, is blown about by anxiety and doubt. Only the wise man, only he whose thoughts are controlled and purified, makes the winds and the storms of the soul obey him.

Tempest-tossed souls, wherever ye may be, under whatsoever conditions ye may live, know this - in the ocean of life the isles of Blessedness are smiling, and the sunny shore of your ideal awaits your coming. Keep your hand firmly upon the helm of thought. In the bark of your soul reclines the commanding Master; He does but sleep; wake Him. Self-control is strength; Right Thought is mastery; Calmness is power.

Say unto your heart, "Peace, be still!"

Afterword

Troward and Allen understood that each individual is endowed with a conscious mind uniquely his. They also understood that we are points of conscious awareness in a universal, subconscious mind. As an extension of the subjective mind that supports and informs reality, each objective or conscious being is a magnet who attracts what he thinks. Your mind is always doing this. The trick is to do it purposefully and with forethought. The upshot is, by directing your thinking, your mind can create the life you want because the universal mind is *your mind,* and the universal mind *is the source of all that is.*

My mother, who was born in 1906, held this to be fact throughout her life. She explained the concept to me fifty years ago when I was a child. She was a reasonably intelligent woman and had attended college, but she was far from what anyone would consider an intellectual. I suspect that if she understood this truth, it was widely known during the first half of the twentieth century.

By the time I was in school, however, the concept of a shared subjective or universal subconscious mind had fallen from grace in spite of many distinguished proponents of the concept, including Carl Jung, the world-renowned psychologist. To my knowledge, no text book contained the theory. I suspect this was so because scientists gained the upper hand who believe to this day that, contrary to the second law of thermal dynamics,[3] life came about and evolved to higher states through a series of incredible accidents. According to

---

[3] This law predicts that the entropy of an isolated system always increases with time, entropy being the measure of the disorder or randomness of energy and matter in a system. Entropy is quite the opposite of evolution.

this theory, intelligence, mind, and awareness are created by electrical impulses jumping from one synapse to another in the brain. On the other hand, Troward apparently believed, as many quantum physicists do today, that what we call intelligence or mind came first and in fact is the ground of being from which physical reality springs. The reality we share, from you and me to quarks and electrons to galaxies and nebula can best be described, they say, as a giant thought. In other words, underlying and giving rise to everything is the universal subjective mind.

Quantum physicists know, for example, that the observer of an experiment can affect the outcome, and this supports Troward's theory. Quite simply, knowledge [thought] possessed by a researcher can determine what happens. An example was reported upon in the June 19, 1995 issue of *Newsweek,* in which a particle of light seemed to "know" what experimenters had in store during a "double slit" experiment.

Double slit experiments have been around a long time. In 1803, Thomas Young demonstrated that light is waves by means of a simple experiment wherein he placed a screen with two parallel slits between a source of light (sunlight coming through a hole in a screen) and a wall. Each slit could be covered with a piece of material. These slits were razor thin, not as wide as the wavelength of the light. When waves of any kind pass through an opening that is not as wide as they are, the waves diffract. This was the case with one slit open. A fuzzy circle of light appeared on the wall.

Alternating bands of light and darkness were seen when both slits were uncovered, the center band being the brightest. This pattern of light and dark resulted from what is known in wave mechanics as interference. Waves overlapped and reinforce each other in some places and in others they canceled each other out. The bands of light on the wall were where one wave crest overlaps another crest. The dark areas were where a crest and a trough met and canceled out each other.

In 1905, Albert Einstein published a paper that proved light also behaves like particles, and he did so by using the photoelectric effect. When light hits the surface of a metal, it jars electrons loose from the atoms in the metal and sends them flying off as though they had been struck by tiny billiard balls. Light is both a wave and particles. This, of course, is a paradox, which according to Newtonian physics cannot be.

Now let's take a look at an experiment in which what the person conducting the experiment knows or doesn't know [i.e., what he thinks and believes] changes the outcome. We set up the double slit experiment this time using a photon gun that fires only one photon at a time. In this case[4] both slits were open and a detector was used to determined which slit a photon passed through. A record was made of where each one hit. Only one photon was shot at a time, so there could be no interference. As a researcher would expect, the photons did not make the zebra pattern.

Now comes the twilight zone part. When the detector was turned off, and it was not known which slit a photon passed through, the zebra pattern appeared.

Noble-winning physicist Richard Feynman calls this the "central mystery" of quantum mechanics, that something as intangible as knowledge — in this case, which slit a photon went through — changes something as concrete as a pattern on a screen.

---

[4] This case is summarized from an article entitled, "Faster Than What?" that can be found in the June 19, 1995 issue of *Newsweek*

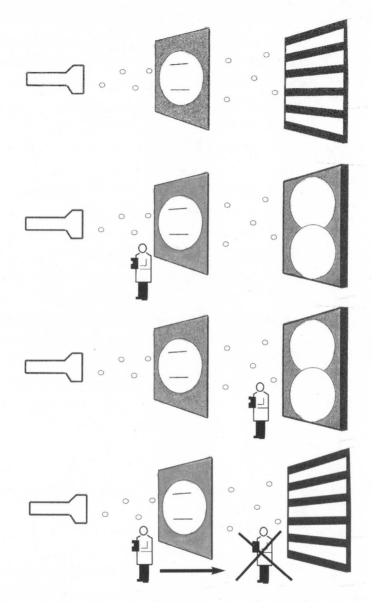

Apparently Thomas Troward was right that time does not exist in the subatomic realm of thought. In this experiment, photons are fired one at a time. If the researcher does not know which slot each photon passes through, a zebra pattern is formed indicating interference as taken place. If the researcher knows which slot each passes through, the zebra pattern disappears. It makes no difference whether the measurement is taken before or after a photon passes the slots, or if it is taken before and then erased. The result is the same. The researcher's knowledge or lack of knowledge is what causes the difference.

Thought that remains inside a person's head would be incapable of having any effect whatsoever. Yet thought in the form of knowledge of which slit a proton passed through does have an effect — as one who subscribes to Allen's and Troward's point of view would expect. The conscious mind determines the actions of the subjective or subconscious mind.

This means that if we believe in our conscious mind we are poor, this will become imprinted on the universal subconscious mind and it will take action to create (or maintain) the circumstances that make this true. If we believe we're rich, it will take action to create or maintain the circumstances that create this opposite reality. Either way, no value judgment is involved. The universe works by laws. It doesn't judge. As Jesus said, "[Your Father in heaven] causes his sun to rise on the evil and the good, and sends rain on the righteous and the unrighteous." (Matthew 5:45)

Consider a hypnotist in action. He puts a subject's objective mind to sleep in order to bypass it and communicate directly with the subconscious mind. This way the subject can be led to believe that he or she is a dog or a chicken, and made to behave accordingly, even though the very idea of this is absurd. The bottom line message is that our reality is created by our thoughts and beliefs.

One could conclude, then, that thinking positive thoughts would be all that's necessary to create a life of joy and abundance. But this falls just short of the truth for a couple of reasons. First, the thoughts and beliefs of others can help us achieve our goals, but it follows that the thoughts and beliefs of others can interfere with and negate the positive ones we pump into the subconscious. Second, and perhaps this is the biggest factor, we are not always aware of our own beliefs, which makes changing them problematic.

This leads to a difference I see in current metaphysical thinking compared to that of a hundred years ago. The idea remains that humanity shares a subconscious mind. The difference between then and now has to do with how the *conscious* mind is structured. Most metaphysicians now believe that the conscious mind is divided into two parts: a conscious portion and an unconscious portion.

The conscious mind is where our attention remains most of the time while we're awake. It's here we're aware of what is going on around us. We touch, taste or see something. Impulses travel along nerves to the brain. An event takes place. Let's say we take a bite of a chocolate bar and immediately recognize the flavor. That's the conscious mind at work. To identify the flavor, the conscious mind called upon the memory of the taste of chocolate that's stored in the unconscious portion.

What other functions does the unconscious part of the conscious mind perform? Let's say you get into your car to go somewhere. You turn the key, you release the brake, you drive. You don't have to think much about what you're doing. You may drive along thinking about something else and take a turn that you would normally take even though you're going somewhere else and shouldn't take that turn today. After a few blocks you realize you're on the wrong road. You were led astray by the unconscious, programmed part of you.

Think about it and you'll realize that the unconscious part of your conscious mind is programmed very much like a computer. Remember the first time you got behind the wheel? When you turned the key and released the brake you had to pay close attention to every detail in order to make the automobile operate smoothly. You had to watch all the buttons, people, stoplights and so on. But over the months and years that you've been driving, your conscious mind made all those details a part of you. They slipped into the unconscious part of your conscious mind as surely as a computer program is loaded onto a hard drive. Thomas Troward understood this to a degree. You may recall that he wrote about habits and the "grooves of thought" etched into the brain. But it seems to me he may have underestimated the power habitual thinking can have on our lives.

The truth is, all the pieces of information you've come in contact with in this life are stored in the unconscious part of your conscious mind, including information that in a practical sense you've forgotten or never fully understood. Erroneous information is there. For example, as a child perhaps your parents said, "People in our family are cursed with a tendency to be overweight. All you have to do is look at food and it goes straight to your hips. There's nothing you can do about it." Or maybe they said, "Nobody in this family ever got rich. It's just not meant to be. So you might as well resign yourself to a life of being poor." Your parents didn't know about Thomas Troward or James Allen, much less subscribe to their beliefs. So in the unconscious part of your conscious mind today may be the beliefs that because you're a Jones or a Johnson or a Smith, you are destined to have a weight problem or to struggle when it comes to money. You didn't question the information when it was programmed in because it came from someone in authority. But it's still there and it's keeping you from a life of joy because as long as those beliefs are in the unconscious part of your conscious mind they are being

Cosmic Mind

Subconscious Minds Merge

Individual Subconscious

Unconscious

Conscious Mind

According to the teachings of the School of Metaphysics in Windyville, Missouri, seven levels of mind exist. Rather than raise questions beyond the scope of this book, however, I have kept things simple by showing only five in this representation. We each have a conscious mind that includes an unconscious portion. At a deep level we have our own subconscious mind. This merges with that of others and ultimately with the universal or cosmic mind. Troward referred to all but the conscious mind as the subjective.

impressed upon a shared subconscious mind that's duty bound to bring them into reality.

You aren't necessarily doomed, however, to suffer financial woe for the rest of your life or to have to buy your clothes at Big and Tall. By bringing that information out of your unconscious, recalling where it came from, looking at it rationally and subjecting it to analysis, the erroneous beliefs can be released. In other words, you can deprogram your unconscious. It will probably help if you will say what's programmed into you out loud, perhaps to a therapist or friend, because this will bring home to you how outrageous, silly and illogical these thoughts usually are. Until you go through this procedure, you're not going to get good long term results simply by imagining what you want and holding it in your mind. The old beliefs must be dispelled or they will undermine your efforts and return conditions to the way they were. This is why posthypnotic suggestions usually don't last. The hypnotist can bypass your conscious mind (both the conscious and the unconscious parts) and tell the subconscious you no longer like that bloated, overstuffed feeling after meals — that after a small amount of food you feel completely satisfied. And for a while this will work. But unless such suggestions are regularly reinforced, they are going to wear off because the belief that you are doomed to be overweight for life is still with you, and eventually it's going regain the upper hand.

Let's say you spend time in self-analysis and remember Aunt Jane impressing upon you the fat curse of the Johnson family. As a result, you are able to reprogram yourself. Now the time has come to move on to other unconscious issues that may be holding you back. Try tuning in to your moment-to-moment stream of consciousness and observing what makes you worried, anxious, resentful, uptight, afraid, angry, and so on. Ask yourself why you reacted as you did. If you retrace what you felt back to its cause, in most cases you'll come to a particular variety of fear, and a fear is a form of belief.

Fears usually can be grouped under one of six headings: the fear of poverty (or failure), the fear of criticism, of ill health, of the loss of love, of old age and of death.

I've listed the fear of poverty (failure) first, because in many ways it can be the most debilitating. Traits develop that bring it about. For example, are you a procrastinator? An underlying fear of failure is probably the root cause and can be counted upon to produce that result.

Are you overly cautious? Do you see the negative side of every circumstance, or stall for the "right time" before taking action? Do you worry (that things will not work out), have doubts (generally expressed by excuses or apologies about why you probably won't be able to perform), suffer from indecision (which leads to someone else, or circumstances, making the decision for you)?

Are you indifferent? This generally manifests as laziness or a lack of initiative, enthusiasm or self control.

Step back and listen for internal voices that say "can't" or "don't" or "won't" or "too risky" or "why bother?"

How do you get rid of them? Bring them out into the open. Talk about them. Maybe even shout about them. See how ridiculous they are, and then shoo them away. The one thing in life over which you have control is your thoughts. You may not be able to control what thoughts arise, but you can decide whether to discard one or keep it.

What about the other fears? They're to be discarded in the

same manner. If you suffer from fear of criticism, for example, it probably came about as a result of a parent or sibling who constantly tore you down to build himself up. You'll know this is a problem if you are overly worried about what others might think, if you lack poise, are self-consciousness or extravagant. Why extravagant? Because of the voice which says you need to keep up with the Jones. You must rid yourself of inner voices that tell you to think even twice about what others will say. Simply eliminate them.

What about the fear of ill health?

To rid yourself of this, it should be enough to know that what you worry about happens. Ever noticed that it's the people who talk about illness, worry about illness, are preoccupied with this or that possible illness, think they feel a pain here or there or were exposed to some germ, who are precisely the people who stay sick most of the time? The power of suggestion is at work.

How about the fear of the loss of love? This one manifests itself in the form of jealousy and is self-fulfilling like the others. The person you try so hard to hang onto feels smothered, with the result that you end up pushing them away. Instead, give them love, but give them room. It they leave you, they would have done so anyway. You can now move on to a truly meaningful relationship.

Next is the fear of old age. This is closely connected to the fear of ill health and the fear of poverty because these are the conditions a person really is concerned about deep down. The power of suggestion is hard at work here, too. If you think you're too old to do this or that, you will indeed be too old. It's been said that our bodies don't wear out, they rust out. So keep moving. Take a brisk walk for an hour a day. Use the treadmill. Go to a health club and take aerobics classes.

Now we've come to that final bugaboo, the fear of death. To borrow a phrase from Franklin Roosevelt, when it comes to death, there's nothing to fear but fear itself. Consider the millions who have had near death experiences and are no longer afraid to die. They're convinced they'll be greeted by loved ones who have gone before. They look forward to being bathed once again in the all-encompassing light which many have described as total, unconditional love. Most do not expect to experience pain. It has been reported by many that the spirit exits the body the instant it looks as though death is inevitable.

Only a handful who have had hell-like experiences are worried about what they may encounter in the nonphysical world. These folks need to know what you are coming to understand. Each of us creates his own reality. We experience what we expect to experience, what we think we deserve, what we believe will happen. If we expect hell, the hell we believe we deserve is the hell we will get. If we expect heaven, our vision of heaven is what we will have. You are what you are and who you are because of your thoughts. Your thoughts can lead you to a life of fulfillment and joy or they can lead you to a life of sorrow and disappointment.

Okay. That's what to do about your own thoughts and beliefs. What about the thoughts and beliefs of others? What about the effect they can have on your personal reality?

I'll be blunt. If you have negative people around you, people who don't believe in you or that a better life is possible, the best thing you can do is put some distance between yourself and them. Move on. Leave them behind so you'll be out of their sight and out of their thoughts. If no way exists to get away at present, it will be best for you *not* to share your goals and aspirations with them. Once they know what you are trying to create for yourself, they're in position to think and say, "That will never happen. It's impossible." In doing so, their thoughts and words almost certainly will have a negative effect.

Regardless of what others may or may not think, you can create your world by employing the secrets of personal alchemy revealed here. Using them, you can create a paradise on earth and enter the kingdom heaven so often spoken of by Jesus. Joy, abundance and good health are within your grasp.

The time has come to take control of your mind and attract what you truly want. So let's review the steps. First, you need to *ask*. As Jesus said, "Ask and it will be given." So decide what you want, write it down, ask for it, and post this request on the mirror you look into every morning. Second, *believe* it is already yours. Again, as Jesus said, "Whatever you ask for in prayer, believe that *you have received it,* and it *will* be yours."[5] Third, feel good about what you have received. Be grateful. Constantly monitor your thoughts by monitoring your feelings. If you start to feel bad, switch gears. Focus on what makes you feel good and make good feelings a habit, knowing the universe will create the outward circumstances to support your pleasant thoughts.

Remember, today is the first day of the rest of your life. The past is history. You can use your thoughts and feelings to create the life of abundance you dare to imagine.

Stephen Hawley Martin
March, 2007

---

[5] Mark 11:24. The italics are mine for emphasis.